Beat
the
Street

A Trader's Guide to Consistently
Scoring in the Markets

Adrian Manz

HARRIMAN HOUSE LTD

3A Penns Road
Petersfield
Hampshire
GU32 2EW
GREAT BRITAIN

Tel: +44 (0)1730 233870
Email: enquiries@harriman-house.com
Website: www.harriman-house.com

Copyright © Harriman House Ltd
First published in Great Britain in 2013 by Harriman House.
Published as *Around the Horn: A Trader's Guide To Consistently Scoring In The Markets* in United States 2003, 2007 by Stilwell & Company.

The right of Adrian Manz to be identified as the Author has been asserted in accordance with the Copyright, Design and Patents Act 1988.

ISBN: 9780857192790

British Library Cataloguing in Publication Data
A CIP catalogue record for this book can be obtained from the British Library.

All rights reserved; no part of this publication may be reproduced, stored in a retrieval system, or transmitted in any form or by any means, electronic, mechanical, photocopying, recording, or otherwise without the prior written permission of the Publisher. This book may not be lent, resold, hired out or otherwise disposed of by way of trade in any form of binding or cover other than that in which it is published without the prior written consent of the Publisher.

No responsibility for loss occasioned to any person or corporate body acting or refraining to act as a result of reading material in this book can be accepted by the Publisher or by the Author.

Hh Harriman House

Contents

About the Author iv

CHAPTER 1. INTRODUCTION 1

CHAPTER 2. THE MENTAL GAME 6
Traders and Athletes 6
Can You Ever be too Confident? 7
Do You Hate to Lose? 9
Does Anyone Know the Score? 11
Summary 11

CHAPTER 3. GROUND RULES 12
Follow the Markets 13
Know Your Market 14
Create a Scan List 17
Scan for Pattern Entries 20
Stop Losses 23
Summary 25

CHAPTER 4. EXPANSION OF RANGE AND VOLUME 26
Big Lots 29
National Fuel Gas 30
Transoceanic Limited 31
Canadian Natural Resources 32
Community Health Systems 33
BRE Properties Inc. 34
Summary 35

CHAPTER 5. EXTENSION REVERSALS 36
Symbol Companhia De Bebidas 38
Gap Inc. 39
Valeant Pharmaceuticals 40
Ashland Inc. 41
Omnicom 42
Abbott Labs 43
Summary 44

CHAPTER 6. GAP EXTENSIONS 45
Ensco PLC 47
Health Care REIT Inc. 48
Mosaic 49
Big Lots 50
Companhia de Bebidas das Americas 51
Moody's Corp. 52
Summary 53

CHAPTER 7. EXPANSION-OF-RANGE REVERSALS 54
Anglogold Ashanti LTD 56
Archer Daniels Midland Co. 57
Baxter Pharmaceuticals 58
Celanese Corp. 59
Cimarex Energy Co. 60
Westlake Chemical Corp. 61
Summary 62

CHAPTER 8. EXPANSION-OF-RANGE-AND-VOLUME CONSOLIDATIONS 63
Aeropostale 65
Edwards Lifesciences 66
Nuskin Enterprises 67
Lennox International 68
Jacobs Engineering Group Inc. 69
Ashland Inc. 70
Summary 71

CHAPTER 9. RATIO PULLBACKS 72
FTI Consulting 75
American Tower Corp 76
BorgWarner 77
Companhia Brasileira 78
Yum Brands 79
Cabot Oil & Gas 80
Summary 81

CHAPTER 10. KINGS AND QUEENS 82
Terex Corporation 84
Ethan Allen Interiors 85
FTI Consulting 86
Crown Castle International Corp. 87
Hospitality Properties Trust 88
Agilent 89
Summary 90

CHAPTER 11. DEFERRED SET-UPS 91
New Oriental Education 93
Devry Inc. 94
Monster Beverage Corp 95
Brookdale Senior Living Inc. 96
Carter Inc. 97
Royal Bank of Canada 98
Basic Energy 99
Summary 100

CHAPTER 12. OPENING-GAP REVERSALS	**101**
Urban Outfitters	103
Aetna Inc	108
American Water Works Inc	110
Best Buy	112
Harris Corp	114
Western Digital Corp	116
Summary	117
CHAPTER 13. CONSOLIDATION BREAKS	**118**
Kinder Morgan Energy Partners Ltd	120
Sonic Automotive Inc	121
FMC Technologies	122
Cameron International Corp	124
Baxter Pharmaceuticals Inc	125
Monster Beverage Corp	126
Summary	127
CHAPTER 14. MOMENTUM REVERSALS	**128**
Kinder Morgan Energy Partners Ltd	129
Target Stores	131
Procter & Gamble	132
Domino's Pizza	134
Allergan Inc	136
Lennar Corp	137
Bunge Limited	138
CHAPTER 15. KEEPING SCORE	**140**
Lexmark	142
Cypress Semiconductor	145
Limited Brands	147
Mosaic	149
Lennox	151
Valeant Pharmaceuticals	153
Global Payments	155
Analysing Results	157
Summary	159
CHAPTER 16. CLOSING THOUGHTS	**160**

About the Author

Dr Adrian Manz earns his living as a professional analyst and stock trader. A successful professional equities trader since 1998, he is the author of two books on the subject and the publisher of the *Around The Horn Intraday Trading Plan*, a nightly blueprint for the actions he plans to take in the markets on the following day. Dr Manz is president of Peterson/Manz Trading Inc. and the co-founder of **TraderInsight.com**. He is dedicated to providing trader education to anyone who is looking to add a new view of the markets to their repertoire. Dr Manz is frequently invited to be a keynote speaker at trading events and is regularly interviewed about his trading style on television, radio, the web and in leading industry magazines. Dr Manz is a graduate of the prestigious Peter F. Drucker Graduate School of Management and the School of Behavioral and Organizational Sciences at Claremont Graduate School. He and his wife Dr Julie Peterson-Manz live and work in Pacific Palisades, California.

CHAPTER 1. Introduction

I HAVE EARNED MY LIVING as a full-time professional equities trader for the past 15 years. I can say without hesitation that it has been a fascinating journey. Those years have been characterised by constant learning, self-discovery and professional, psychological and emotional growth. A career as a trader has been different to virtually anything else I might have pursued. It involves constantly questioning conventional wisdom about allocating resources to the markets. The actions taken by investors run counter to those that are taken by a professional trader. Long-term investors are interested in factors that are completely irrelevant in shorter time frames. While investors need to focus on the probable outcome over a long time horizon, successful traders are focused on what will happen *today*. The ability to predict what will happen over the next few hours defines success. The methods I employ have served me very well in fostering this ability; the tools that I use to accomplish my success are described in detail in this book.

Trading also involves a significant psychological challenge. It is not enough to learn to think differently from an investor. A trader also needs to reframe what defines success and failure. Success is typically associated with winning; failure with losing. The parallels in trading would be making or losing money. Yet these most basic measures of accomplishment, unless radically rethought, will only undermine a trader's ability to succeed. Winning feels good. Losing feels bad. Most human beings are hardwired to avoid the latter emotion. In trading this translates into snatching at winners and self-denial over losers; and that spells certain failure. Those who wash out of the game usually do so because of this simple psychology. It means they never grasp the most basic axiom of successful trading: let your winners run and cut your losers short.

Taking many small gains and a few large losses is a quick route to ruin. Trading demands that those who hope to persevere engage in a psychological paradigm shift. My personal paradigm is quite effective. I know that my trading plan generates great results over time. Whether I gain or lose money today has no bearing on that fact. I judge my success or failure by a simple benchmark: whether or not I followed my plan to the letter. If I did, I succeeded. If I did not, I failed. This is true whether I made or lost money on the session. In this book, I will show the reader the exact chart patterns that I have used to plan each and every trade I have taken over the past 15 years.

To be a successful trader you must love the great game that is the stock market. You must be on a constant quest to hone your skills at the game. There are no good or bad days – just days with varying degrees of opportunity and more or less success in the implementation of a trading plan. My perception of the market is ever-evolving. I see things very differently today than I did back in the 1990s. The differences that I perceive are very real. A dozen years ago opportunity presented itself in a manner very similar to a fast-action video game. If you showed up ready to play the game, you had a good chance of turning a profit. All that was needed was a sound strategy and nerves of steel. In the 1990s, I would go to work in the morning, assess the direction of the pre-market futures, and get ready to capitalise on any momentum that correlated with what the broader markets and sectors were doing. While this style of trading still represents a small portion of my daily activity, the majority of what I do is the result of careful planning. This text will cover all of what I do, from carefully planned to semi-discretionary trading. There is no secret here – the only thing that cannot be conveyed in this book is the hand of experience in steering the selection and execution process. The only way to gain that insight is by becoming a student of the patterns and the markets, and putting in the time to become an expert in each.

Trading profitably requires an understanding of the markets, strategy and yourself. My trading has evolved significantly over the years, as has my thinking. I have developed a methodology that relies on market dynamics, represented in easy-to-spot patterns, to get me in front of trading opportunities with a high probability of a successful outcome. I prepare for tomorrow's trading after the close of trading today. The results of this fastidious planning have been impressive, with a track record over the past six years that does not include a single losing month. There are losing days, and losing weeks, but month over month the strategies that I will describe in this book have kept me in business while many of my contemporaries have been less fortunate.

My unique view of the markets has led to success in the very difficult trading environment of the late 1990s and the 2000s. My focus on the cyclicality of markets and the impact that the movement of broader markets and sectors have on the behaviour of individual stocks differentiates what I do from the actions of the majority. Figure 1.1 below is a simple representation of market cyclicality. This cyclicality needs to be on a trader's mind every day if there are to be profits on the horizon. Each of the patterns in this book is designed to capitalise on known characteristics of each of the phases of the market cycle.

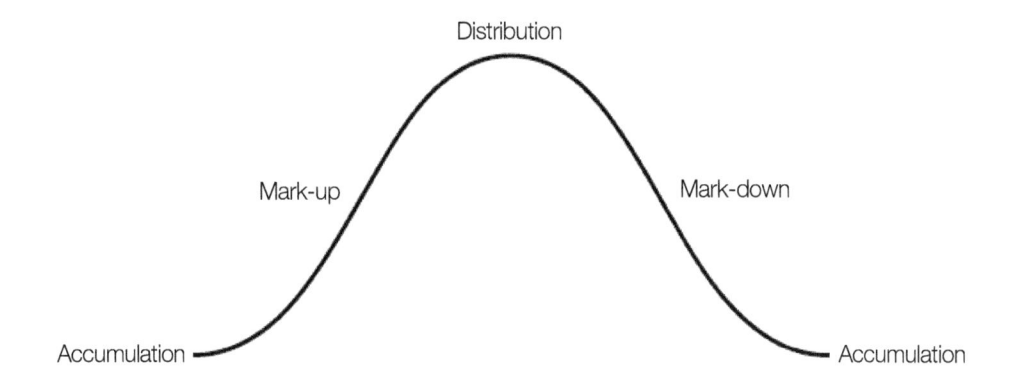

[Figure 1.1: A bell-curve diagram showing the market cycle phases — Accumulation (left), Mark-up (rising side), Distribution (top), Mark-down (falling side), Accumulation (right).]

FIGURE 1.1

Markets move through a known rotation of phases identified as accumulation, mark-up, distribution, and mark-down. During the accumulation and distribution phases, markets move sideways and typically offer only a few, very specialised types of trading opportunity. These are also the periods during which trading can be the most difficult and risky. Most of the patterns that I trade avoid the accumulation and distribution phases in favor of the mark-up and mark-down phases. These phases represent the times that a market is trending. They also serve to put traders on the path of opportunity. There will always be trading instruments in a mark-up or mark-down phase, so there are always opportunities to be had. There are no periods during which every stock in the market is in the exact same phase, so there is never any reason to force a trade.

The ability to find real opportunities, plan entries and exits based on a sound rationale, and then have the determination to execute your plan are what is required to succeed. Everything but that determination is contained in this book; and I believe that after the reader has reviewed the results in Chapter 15, as well as the complete spreadsheet of every trade planned and executed since 2005, the determination to follow the plan will be forthcoming as well. The latter spreadsheets can be found in the members' area of my website **www.traderinsight.com**. The members' area also contains hundreds of videos that reinforce the ideas presented in the book. It also provides additional insight into what is happening in the current market, and where additional opportunities for profit can be found.

My goal with this book is to teach the reader a consistent and conservative methodology for trading the financial markets. I have used the exact patterns and methods presented here for 15 years to generate consistent trading results. Consistency is the key to survival in this game. I believe that by studying each chapter carefully, and internalising the spirit, cause and effect of each pattern, you will be better positioned to achieve consistency than 99% of the people who attempt to trade for a living.

I know that no admonition to the contrary will keep most readers from skipping the section on psychology and discipline and flipping first to the patterns. But I promise that becoming consistent is about more than just pattern recognition. A trader needs to understand his or her personal psychology, and develop a discipline that takes that psychology into account. Many books out there suggest that they will teach you how to trade. What they do not suggest is that they will teach you how to trade profitably. This is because the authors know that it is impossible to teach someone to run a profitable trading business simply by reading a few hundred pages of a book. Unless you happen to share a virtually identical psychology, aptitude and temperament with the author, you stand no more chance of becoming profitable by reading a trading text than you do of becoming a master chef by reading a cookbook. You need to teach yourself to trade.

Part of that process is developing an understanding of your personal relationship with money, profit, loss, success and failure. The process of becoming successful includes self-discovery. The psychology section of this book is there to help you with this and to assist you in developing habits and behaviours that will allow you to profit from the methods I employ in my own trading. Carefully reading and considering the personal impact of the ideas I will present in that chapter (Chapter 2) will help you become a better trader and put you in the right frame of mind to implement the strategies that are presented later.

All that being said, I hope that you find the ideas presented in *Beat the Street: A Trader's Guide to Consistently Profiting in the Markets* as useful as I have. It is my sincere hope that the reader can learn to profit from my ideas for the next 15 years, just as I have for the past 15.

As a buyer of the printed book of *Beat the Street*, you can download the full eBook free of charge. Simply point your smartphone or tablet camera at this QR code or go to:
ebooks.harriman-house.com/beatthestreet

CHAPTER 2.
The Mental Game

Psychology is one of the most important factors in the success of a trader. Yet most people flip right past any section discussing psychology in the trading books and periodicals they buy. Traders want information they can read today and make money with tomorrow. They love chapters about profitable chart patterns and hope that they will discover the holy grail in the techniques they read about. But if there is a holy grail, the place to find it is in a thorough understanding of what makes us tick. A trader's personal psychology, including all of the strengths and weaknesses he or she brings to work every morning, is the key to unlocking a consistently profitable career.

There is a simple fact with which every trader needs to come to grips: you will never master the markets until you master yourself. It will not matter how many books you buy, courses you take or personal coaches you hire. If you are not in touch with what makes you tick, the market will remain an enigma. No amount of money, time or training will allow you to trade with anything other than the odds afforded to those who seek their thrills wagering on games of chance. The good news is that personal psychology is something individuals have been successfully able to master. It is what makes any competitive, energetic and motivated person capable of fulfilling his or her dream.

Traders and Athletes

Great athletes are masters of their sport in large part because they are self-aware. Of course they have athletic ability. But plenty of people who could not connect with the ball if their life depended on it also have ability. The great players know their psychological boundaries and are masters of the balancing act that keeps skill and emotion working together instead of as opposing forces. They are not overconfident as they approach their sport. They are not afraid to fail. And they definitely do not keep a running total of successes and failures churning through their head. Instead, they strategise around their own psychology. That might mean trying to maximise their defensive or team play and having a low number of individual scores, or focusing on maximum offense every time, knowing that this will result in a low average but a potentially high number of personal wins. Whatever the secret to their success, it emanates from a confluence between the needs of the person inside and the actions of the person playing the game. The same awareness and psychological balance that make for a great athlete make for a great trader. Neither can achieve success without balance, and both must overcome psychological obstacles on the road to success.

I think there are three general psychological road blocks common to struggling traders. They are overconfidence, a fear of losing and mental bean-counting. We will take a quick look at these. As you read the following sections, think about the impact each of these has had on your career in the markets. When you get to the point that each of these is held in check, you will find trading for a living to be a much more profitable and relaxed experience.

Can You Ever be too Confident?

Successful traders tend to have a public persona that exudes simple confidence. That confidence is the product of experience in the markets. They are confident because they have witnessed first-hand what works, what does not work, and what the odds are for success in any given situation. They know that their opinion is worth something because of their experience, but are still in touch with the fact that they are just offering an opinion.

By contrast, the least successful traders I have known exude *over*confidence. They label the successes of others as insignificant. They are quick to explain what 'real traders' would or would not do. They brag about their successes and claim that their losses are not worth discussing. I have known many of these people. Generally they are suffering from an attribution error. They feel that to be successful, you have to think and act successful. In the process, they overcompensate for their lack of experience and put themselves in a position of dissonance. Such dissonance will be resolved only when they give up trading and look for another profession. For them, cognitive consonance will be achieved only when they can explain to their friends that trading is for suckers and is a game that cannot be won. The detrimental impact of overconfidence on the ultimate prosperity of traders is supported by academic research conducted in the United States.

If you are overconfident, you will likely overtrade. If you overtrade, you will decimate your return rate with high transaction costs. You will also make the wrong trades. Research conducted at the University of California, Berkeley and the University of California, Davis found that overconfidence led to overtrading with solid positions being closed in favour of less profitable ones. The study found that individuals who traded 45% more actively than their counterparts actually reduced returns by 2.5% per annum. I believe that this emanates, once again, from the desire of the overconfident trader to demonstrate how exceptional his skills are. Taking losses looks and feels bad. Booking gains looks and feels good. So the only proven formula for success – cut your losers short and let your winners run – goes out the window. Ultimately, these traders wind up with a portfolio full of their worst trades.

I believe that the solution to this problem is to trade according to a very clearly defined plan. By building discipline, traders can learn to avoid the pitfall of constantly firing off trades in an effort to beat the market. I can say from my own early experience in this business that shooting from the hip almost inevitably leads to shooting oneself in the foot.

I avoid overtrading by creating a detailed plan every night. This covers one to six of what I consider to be the best trades for the next day in NYSE-listed securities. When the market is trending, I don't see the excitement other traders do, but my returns are steady and my statement of profits and losses heads in the right direction. When the market is tough, I still manage to keep a consistent rate of return. I am not in this business as a hobby. I am not in it for the excitement. I am here because I love trading and because my methodology allows me to make a living at it. I know traders who take upward of 200 trades per week and cannot even tell me what their rate of return is. They seem to enjoy the sport of it. I choose to run my business a different way. I know exactly what I will trade every day. I have a concise plan and a detailed log that I can review at a moment's notice. I know how my plan is performing and can easily ascertain why. I know the methodology works, and I can increase my dollar return at any time by increasing share size. This is truly the most beautiful thing about trading for a living. Once you have found what works for you, you can double your income simply by doubling share size. And you can do this over and over again. This is my comfort zone. I am inherently conservative, and this approach matches my psychology while providing me the opportunity to make a living doing what I love. Please be sure to review the actual example of a day of my trading plan and log in Chapter 15 after you have had a chance to become familiar with the patterns.

Do You Hate to Lose?

If your mindset is dominated by the fear of losing money, it is a virtual certainty that you will lose over and over again. Paradoxically fear leads to the same cognitive errors and subsequent trading mistakes as overconfidence. Fear of loss, not greed, is another reason traders stay with losing positions and dump winners. Although this seems counter-intuitive, perhaps an example will convince you.

Say we have a trader whom we will call 'Jim'. Trader Jim takes both long and short trades and tries to follow a plan every trading day. Jim knows that trading is not an exact science, and that losses are part of the business. Nevertheless, like all of us he would like to keep those losses as small as possible. Along comes a long trade in XYZ Corporation, which Jim takes according to his plan. The stock moves up, briefly consolidates just short of his profit target, and then moves sharply lower. Jim suspects that the trade is probably going to bounce. Since a bounce is not part of his plan, he exits the trade at the stop loss. He then cannot take his eyes off the screen. He watches in disgust as XYZ turns around right at the stop loss and begins to head higher. Jim is upset, but when XYZ trades through the entry price again, he takes the trade. After this second entry, the stock again reverses to the stop loss. Jim once more exits, only to watch XYZ reverse and move higher. Jim's strategy only calls for first and second entry, but the rest of his day is dominated by XYZ as he watches it trade higher and lower, with just about every exit looking better than his own.

So what has Jim learned from the experience? If he has balanced his psychological needs with the trading system he uses, he is probably patting himself on the back for following his plan: what matters is trading in a disciplined fashion, sticking to a rigorous and tested outline, even if on occasion events go against you. If not, he has learned that to violate his plan is to prosper. In future, he will be prepared to do just that, even though nine times out of ten it will spell ruin. But fear has got a hold of him; doubt has eaten away at the foundations of his plan; and he – like so many traders before him – is ready to slip down the road to disaster. The next time XYZ trades slightly up, he will sell rather than hold in accordance with his plan. He is too worried it will drop. He will do the same with other stocks. He will miss out repeatedly on significant price rises when they do come, and much-needed profit; grasping at small gains in order to have something, he will let the bulk of profit slip through his fingers.

Traders like this are afraid of losing. They fail to adequately address that fear in the construction and application of their trading strategy, and their entire career is dominated by it. If you find yourself letting losses run and cutting profits short, if overconfidence isn't to blame then you are probably allowing fear to control your trading. After all, profits feel good and losses feel bad. Thus, some will always take profits, however small, as soon as a position moves in their favour. I have seen traders take progressively smaller gains out of the market until a profitable trade barely covered commissions. The flip side is that losses are allowed to become larger, or even worse, are added to a portfolio of long-term holdings made up entirely of 'short-term' losers. Why? Because not taking the loss means not losing. Thus the avoidance of the feared outcome becomes a self-fulfilling prophecy in which the ultimate result is the fear being realised in the form of emotional and financial failure.

If you laugh at the idea of fear impacting your trades, that might be a good sign that it is overconfidence instead which threatens you. Every trader must navigate between the Syclla of overconfidence and the Charbydis of fear if they are to be successful.

Does Anyone Know the Score?

A great athlete never has a bad game – he just has games. Stepping on to the field does not involve a mental recalculation of his statistics. It does not mean remembering the last time he faced this particular opponent. And it certainly does not entail remembering how many times in the past he has failed to score. The same is true of profitable traders.

To succeed in the business of trading, you have to get to work every morning and be able to approach the markets *tabula rasa*. Fixating on previous losses will serve only to elevate the fear that prevents you from trading your plan. Focusing on a few days of extraordinary gains will bring out overconfidence, and over trading, and turn a strong profit and loss history into a fiasco.

I recommend not even counting your money. Obviously, we all need to draw our paycheques. And we need to remain aware of how our plans are playing out. But constantly counting the beans will not fill the jar any quicker. I look at my returns quarterly. Any shorter time frame causes me to focus unnecessarily on short-term performance. And once we worry constantly about performance, the game is essentially over.

Summary

By any account, I have not covered the entire impact that personal psychological makeup has on decisions made in the markets. The three topics discussed here – overconfidence, fear, performance anxiety – are simply those that I feel are common to almost all of us, and yet are almost never properly examined. We are all carrying baggage that fuels these and other problems in the field of trading. I strongly suggest that before reading any further, you stop to think about such roadblocks to success that you have constructed, and the possible reasons and solutions for them.

CHAPTER 3.
Ground Rules

As far as I am concerned, the most important factor in becoming a successful trader is learning to stick to a plan. We have all heard the anecdote *"Plan the trade . . . trade the plan"* but most of us find it nearly impossible to do so, even if we invest tremendous sweat equity in the plan's construction.

I think that this inclination to second guess and revise our planning emanates from a desire to avoid risk. Too often as traders, we think that we recognise an event that led to a previous loss unfolding again, and decide that this time, we have the opportunity to emerge victorious. If we are lucky, then the market will slap us on the wrist immediately for straying from a carefully devised plan in favour of acting on a hunch. If we are unlucky, we are rewarded for the behaviour, and it will become increasingly difficult to stay the course. Eventually, this series of events leads to ruin, and my best advice to traders of all levels of experience is to learn to precisely plan, and then flawlessly execute. This is the only path that can lead to an objective understanding of what works and what does not. That objectivity, in turn, leads to a trading psychology that is characterised by courage and conviction. These characteristics foster success.

This chapter will lay the groundwork for developing effective, actionable plans based on the pattern entries detailed in later chapters. Learning to trade by the plan is the first step in becoming a profitable trader.

Follow the Markets

It is entirely possible to trade every day without following market news at all. I do not know, however, that it is plausible to make a living that way. I know traders who will take a position in ABC, XYZ and everything in-between, yet are unable to tell me even the most basic facts about what makes the market tick. They have problems with their profit/loss consistency over time, and it tends to make them move constantly from one methodology to another.

In my opinion, a firm understanding of the broader markets is a precursor to success. As such, I follow a number of market statistics and plot them every day. These facts and figures tell me whether my trading plan is in sync with the market, or if I am relying on something out of the ordinary to move my positions in my favour. I construct my market barometer in both daily and weekly time frames. The format is simple and tracks everything that I feel is important to know. I use the spreadsheet in Figure 3.1 as a means of consolidating the data.

Every trader should construct such a spreadsheet. Include the major market indices and a list of sectors that represent where the money tends to move. The sectors in my table are underliers of the majority of stocks that I trade. If my nightly scan begins generating frequent hits in sectors that I do not follow on this consolidated report, then I either add the sector or delete the stock from the list. My rule is that if I do not understand what the stock's sector is doing, I stay away from the trade no matter how good it looks. This ensures me increased odds of profitability over the long run.

As important as following the markets is, it is also critical to know what the indices are doing. By this, I mean that market internals must be examined to ascertain whether the markets are actually moving or if they are being moved by the great manipulators out there who profit by engineering runs on low volume. I follow basic internals such as advancers, decliners and volume (advancing and declining). I also follow the CBOE Volatility Index (VIX). This index provides a very good indication of whether the broader indices are going to sustain their current motion or reverse and head in the opposite direction.

Indices	Monday	Tuesday	Wednesday	Thursday	Friday
Dow Jones Industrial Avg	13271.64	13203.58	13172.76	13,057	13157.97
NASDAQ-100	2784.33	2772.2	2783.42	2762.02	2778.05
NASDAQ Composite	3076.21	3067.26	3073.67	3053.4	3069.79
S&P 500 Index	1414.75	1412.5	1412.25	1400	1409.75
Russell 2000	816.51	815.36	812.56	806	809.19
Sectors					
Amex Biotechnology Index	1,446.98	1,442.20	1,454.18	1,455.94	1,470.61
AMEX Pharmaceutical Index	359.14	357.75	357.45	357.15	359.32
Amex Computer Hardware Index	365.03	361.46	357.89	352.40	356.66
PHLX Semiconductor	402.29	402.30	399.17	396.66	398.95
Morgan Stanley Consumer Index	821.20	816.51	813.75	808.27	814.19
Consumer Discretionary Index	453.28	452.49	453.68	450.78	454.32
PHLX Gold/Silver Sector	161.05	164.36	168.05	168.41	168.50
S&P Health Care	446.14	444.69	444.73	444.16	447.81
S&P Insurance	190.88	190.55	190.32	188.89	190.17
Morgan Stanley Internet Index	34.77	34.63	34.99	34.90	35.01
CBOE S&P Banks Index	158.59	158.98	158.61	157.28	158.13
NYSE Financial Index	4,597.68	4,613.47	4,607.84	4,569.52	4,585.08
DEUTSCHE BANK ENERGY INDEX	1,241.01	1,238.97	1,240.18	1,226.76	1,231.31
Amex Oil Index	1,238.79	1,234.04	1,237.47	1,225.59	1,231.09
S&P Chemical	345.39	343.97	347.25	341.60	341.40
Internals					
NYSE Advancers	1,315.00	1,297.00	1,174.00	909.00	1,893.00
NYSE Decliners	1,656.00	1,640.00	1,812.00	2,055.00	1,037.00
NYSE Adv/Dec Ratio	0.79	0.79	0.65	0.44	1.83
NYSE Total Volume	550,934.00	640,954.00	600,771.00	592,711.00	515,249.00
Bias					
Market Volatility Index CBOE	14.02	15.02	15.11	15.96	15.18
NYSE Tick Indicator	883.00	(195.00)	(18.00)	(621.00)	838.00
NYSE Arms Indicator	0.87	0.91	0.74	1.67	0.76

FIGURE 3.1 MARKET SNAPSHOT

Know Your Market

I trade primarily New York Stock Exchange-listed securities. While the patterns I rely on will work equally well in any market, I find the NYSE to be more predictable and easier to trade than the NASDAQ. This is not an absolute, and the choice should be made by each trader individually. Trade where you are comfortable. I know traders whose mantra is "if it moves I will trade it". If that works for you, then more power to you. Just realise that the NYSE (even with the advent of the hybrid market) is a different animal to the computerised markets. Each takes some getting used to. Each has benefits. Each certainly has drawbacks.

Using the NYSE OpenBook

If you plan to trade NYSE securities, then a good monthly data feed investment is the NYSE OpenBook which provides indication of the depth and liquidity of the market in any given stock. While not the same as NASDAQ Level II or TotalView, the OpenBook is less subject to gamesmanship, and provides a snapshot of what the market is about to do. There are some general concerns traders should remain aware of when using this tool.

First, the OpenBook provides only the data that represents the specialist on the NYSE. Thus it can sometimes be out of sync with the Level II inside quote. This is particularly true in fast-moving stocks with lots of Electronic Communication Network (ECN) activity.

Second, the OpenBook represents only limit and marketable limit orders on the specialist's book. There is no indication of the number of market orders. Tape-reading is still required if you are interested in knowing where market orders are located and where they are being filled.

Third, the OpenBook may be crossed or locked. If the high bid is above the inside ask, it will be placed at the top of the book in the order of greatest to lowest price. Offers that are placed below the market are put on the book in the same manner. Both types of orders stay on the montage until they are filled. This can be very helpful, since a large buy or sell order above or below the market will be reflected on the OpenBook, and not on the Level II screen, giving traders an indication of buying or selling pressure that is entering the market.

Fourth, short sales and stop-limits are reflected on the book when they are 'elected' and are displayed at the price at which they are eligible for a fill.

Many NASDAQ traders find that they do not like the OpenBook because of the dissimilarities to Level II data. I would say just the opposite. I think that the absence of all the head fakes and market-maker games makes the NYSE OpenBook more valuable than its NASDAQ counterpart. I feel that, just like with any tool, you have to learn how to use it properly. Only then can decisions regarding its utility be made.

Figure 3.2 below shows the manner in which OpenBook data are displayed by the specialist. Note the presence of an offer of significant size priced slightly above the current market. In the absence of a market order to buy 21,400 shares, this stock is about to consolidate or move lower to price liquidity pools. I find that the OpenBook is generally pretty predictable in situations like this. The 21,000 share offer at 55.43 will be filled by the specialist as close to the intraday volume-weighted average price for the stock as possible. The pressure on the OpenBook definitely indicates that, without a substantial buy-side order, the stock will likely move lower.

Name	Size	Bid	Ask	Size	Name
NYOB	300	55.40	55.41	100	NYOB
NYOB	100	55.39	55.42	300	NYOB
NYOB	100	55.38	55.43	21000	NYOB
NYOB	500	55.34	55.45	421	NYOB
NYOB	200	55.33	55.46	13	NYOB
NYOB	100	55.32	55.47	721	NYOB
NYOB	100	55.31	55.48	200	NYOB
NYOB	400	55.29	55.49	400	NYOB
NYOB	100	55.25	55.51	100	NYOB
NYOB	100	55.24	55.53	500	NYOB
NYOB	100	55.20	55.55	100	NYOB
NYOB	300	55.19	55.57	1000	NYOB
NYOB	100	55.18	55.62	1700	NYOB
NYOB	1700	55.15	55.69	500	NYOB
NYOB	100	55.13	55.76	3100	NYOB
NYOB	3100	55.03	55.79	400	NYOB
NYOB	100	55.00	55.80	100	NYOB
NYOB	400	54.76	55.91	20	NYOB
NYOB	100	54.75	56.00	80	NYOB
NYOB	200	54.73	56.05	100	NYOB

FIGURE 3.2 NYSE OPENBOOK

Create a Scan List

In order to trade successfully, you must have a pool of stocks that comprise a list of potential candidates. I create this pool every month and follow some very basic guidelines regarding price, liquidity and trend.

Price

I trade stocks that range between $30 and $120. This provides enough volatility to earn a living, and the requisite stability for my stops to be set within my personal comfort zone.

Liquidity

I construct my list of potential candidates to include stocks trading as few as 400,000 and as many as 4 million shares on average per day. I use a 30-day look-back period to calculate average volume. I find that lower volume generally equates to better volatility and an easier market to predict. This is a personal preference, but you should definitely scrutinise this factor very carefully; the personality of stocks trading less than 400,000 shares can be erratic, while those trading many millions of shares each day can be frustrating.

Trend

Almost every pattern I trade develops in the course of a trend. There are several ways to identify trending stocks, and I generally use the most simple of them. I look at the chart. If a line connecting the lows is moving from the southwest to the northeast corner, the stock is in an uptrend. If a line connecting the highs is moving from the northwest corner to the southeast, then the stock is in a downtrend. If the line moves horizontally from west to east, then the stock is not in a trend and should be avoided.

There are those who find this methodology too simple, or who prefer not to flip through a lot of charts every night. For those individuals there are several alternatives, the best of which is ADX, an indicator of trend strength, coupled with DI+ and DI-, which are indicators of directional bias.

ADX

Developed by Welles Wilder, and described in his 1978 book *New Concepts in Technical Trading Systems*, the ADX indicator measures the strength of an existing trend as well as whether movement exists in the market during one half of an ideal market cycle. I prefer a 10-period ADX, while 14 is the number suggested by Wilder. A calculated ADX under 20 traditionally indicates a non-trending market. A move above 20 may signal the start of an up or downtrend. When ADX begins to fall from a level over 40, it is traditionally interpreted as signalling a potential flattening of the dominant trend. A very extended ADX can be used to indicate that the market is overbought or oversold, but I would advise against using the indicator for this purpose. Markets can maintain extreme readings for a long time, and a strong trend can continue moving indefinitely even if the ADX is well above 40.

DI+ and DI-

Given an ADX of 20 or greater, DI+ and DI- provide insight into which direction the market is moving. Generally speaking, if DI+ is greater than DI- and ADX is greater than 20 and rising, the trend is up. If DI- is greater than DI+ and ADX is greater than 20 and rising, the trend is down.

The derivations of the values are as follows:

- High of the current bar = H
- Low of the current bar = L
- Close of the current bar = C
- High of one bar ago = H1
- Low of one bar ago = L1
- Close of one bar ago = C1

Directional movement (DM) must first be computed. To do this, we have to create a sort of tally for two teams. Label the first team's score DI+, and the second team's DI-. Now compare the current bar's high (H) and low (L) with those of the previous bar, (H1) and (L1) respectively. If H - H1 is greater than L - L1 then place the result of the calculation H - H1 in the DI+ column. If L - L1 is greater than H - H1 then place the result of the calculation L - L1 in the DI- column. Now total each column and divide by the number of cases to get the average.

Next, you must compute the true range (TR) for each of the bars. To calculate true range, take the greatest value of the following computations:

H - L

H - C1

L - C1

Using the same number of bars as you used for the directional movement calculations (I use 10), sum the ATR values and compute the average.

Now, calculate DI+ and DI -

- If DM was up, then DI+ = (+DM ÷ TR)

- If DM was down, then DI- = (-DM ÷ TR)

$$ADX = \frac{(DI+)n - (DI)n}{(DI+)n - (DI)n} \times 100\% \quad n = \text{the number of bars in the look back period}$$

Here, we divide the difference between all the DI numbers by the sum of all the DI numbers, and then multiply by 100 to change the value to a percentage.

As the ADX number becomes larger, the difference between DI+ and DI- will widen, and the trend on a chart will be in the direction of the larger of the two values.

While nearly every piece of trading software computes these values automatically, I suggest that you never apply an indicator to a chart unless you understand it well enough to explain to a friend how its values are calculated and what the results tell you.

Scan for Pattern Entries

Once your scan-list is created, you have the pool of candidates from which to draw daily pattern entries. Update the list as often as is practical, but no less than once per month. The patterns are detailed in the chapters that follow. What we need to establish here are the guidelines for determining entry points, initial profit targets and stop-loss levels.

Entry points are at follow-through confirmation levels. I typically use .10 for stocks under $50 and .15 for those trading at prices above $50. Thus, for a long pattern entry in a $30 stock that requires a breakout above the previous session's high, the trigger price would be (H1 + .10). A short entry with the inverse requirement would trigger at (L1 - .10).

Entry is predicated on the fact that the pattern being considered seems likely to follow through to a profit target that is greater than the potential move to the stop loss. Determining this likelihood is where the art and science of trading collide, but the procedure I use can be roughly quantified as follows:

1. Examine the daily chart to see how much overhead resistance for longs, or support for shorts, will be encountered along the path you expect the stock to follow.
2. Examine the intraday five-minute chart of the stock and determine if there has been significant support or resistance that might impede progress to the target.
3. Calculate the pivot, first and second support, and first and second resistance levels that will characterise trading on the following day (see next section).
4. Establish an initial profit target at or around anticipated overlapping support and resistance zones.
5. Determine a reasonable stop loss based on daily and intraday support and resistance confluence areas.
6. Compare the prices in steps 1–3. If there is significant overlap of values in the path to your profit target, discard the pattern for the following trading day. It is far better to let a set-up go than to try and reason your way through significant price-inflection points.

7. If there does not seem to be a significant obstacle en route to the target, record the potential trade in a journal and define the parameters on paper for the next trading day.

Calculating pivot lines

Each night, we identify market inflection levels known as pivot points. These represent the equilibrium areas around which most of the day's trading activity can be expected to occur. Statistically, a trader has a significantly higher probability of achieving profits when taking the pivot levels into account in assessing technical set-ups. Let's examine the calculations and what each point means.

The *pivot point* (P) is the non-weighted average of yesterday's price action. I refer to P as being non-weighted because the calculation is simply (high + low + close) ÷ 3. By contrast, the *volume-weighted average price* (VWAP) is a calculation that is weighted to reflect all of the day's market action at every conceivable price level. Nevertheless, P is very important for a number of reasons. First, floor traders and market makers use P as a sort of axis around which to base fair price. Second, if the market begins to defy this level as the equilibrium price, its value is critical in developing the support and resistance calculations that floor traders will use to make their markets.

The first level of resistance (R1) is calculated as [(2 × P) - L], while the first support (S1) is [(2 × P) - H]. The results of these calculations provide a set of bands within which floor traders will anticipate containment of price. Price action in the absence of significant news events within these bands represents the 'value' range. Any move that penetrates one of these is what we commonly refer to as a breakout. When this range expansion occurs, off-floor intraday traders become interested and are pulled into the market. The level of activity here determines whether the move will continue to expand, or fizzle.

The second level of resistance (R2) is calculated as [P + (R1 - S1)], while the second support (S2) is [P - (R1 - S1)]. These parameters serve to generate a second set of bands which will, theoretically, contain the newly expanded price action. If a move through these levels is achieved, swing and longer-term traders will be drawn into the market. The level of participation here can result in very significant breakouts, or, once again, a profit-taking fizzle.

Using pivots in the creation of the nightly plan

Assume now that you have done your nightly technical analysis, generated a list of potential trade candidates and calculated pivot points for each. Working under the assumption that each pivot line will generate support or resistance, you should be able to quickly determine whether an anticipated move will be sustainable. For example, if your profit target for an intraday trade is one point, but achieving that level of profit requires the successful penetration of two pivot lines, you may want to rethink your strategy.

Avoiding a loss often involves limiting profits. In this case, a more reasonable initial target may be the first area of pivot resistance (for long trades) or support (for shorts). Given these levels, if the trade still makes sense from a risk/reward vantage point, keep it on your list. Take profits from a portion of your position when the initial target is reached. Allow the rest of your position to continue moving if the other indicators you rely on as decision support tools indicate that the current trend will continue to move in your favour.

Taking the trades

When it comes to the trading day, my philosophy is to think as little as possible. I spend a great deal of time putting together my intraday trading plan, and I have found that I *never* come out ahead when I second guess the set-ups during trading hours. The only exception here is the planning of intraday trades that develop in other stocks based on our interpretation of market conditions, and the intraday relative strength of relevant indices. Intraday patterns are covered in the Intraday Pattern section of this book.

Stop Losses

I use six types of stops in my trading. The one applied to a trade at any given time depends entirely on what the trade has been doing since entry. This makes the topic pretty subjective, but I think it is worth reviewing.

Intraday support and resistance

Setting a stop loss is probably the most important part of creating your nightly plan. Since we only have an educated guess as to what the market will do tomorrow, we need to set our "uncle point" based on price action the day before a trade is to be taken.

I suggest that you use multiple time frames when planning stops. I use a 5 minute chart, since this is what I trade from, and 25-tick and 15 minute charts because they represent greater and smaller views. The actual stop placement is simply a matter of looking for the peaks and valleys on the intraday chart, and determining where prices tend to cluster. One high does not a stop make. Five or ten, however, and a significant part of the day was spent attempting to move through a price level before failure to push through caused price to move away.

Intraday support and resistance is always my first stop, and combined with the pivot points is how I set the initial profit target. If the distance from the entry to the stop is greater than that from the entry to the projected target, I remove the trade from the plan.

The eight-period simple moving average (SMA)

Once I have entered a trade, I maintain my original stop until the stock moves to it or moves substantially in my favour. By substantially, I mean at least 50% of the distance to the target. At this point, I use an eight-period SMA to contain the trend, and a violation of .10 below the SMA as a profit-protecting stop in a trend.

If price starts to consolidate during the uptrend, I use the bottom of the consolidation or the eight-SMA, whichever will keep me in the trade longer. This gives price action room to breathe in the multitude of trendless periods during the day.

Fibonacci retracement zones

If price rapidly moves in favour of the trade, intraday support and resistance and the eight-period SMA will give too much money back to the market for my comfort. When these fortunate situations arise, I use breaks of Fibonacci levels (usually .382 or .618) as exit points. The problem here lies in moves that contain dramatic extensions. In these instances, even the .382 level can be too far away to be practical.

Reversal of two closes

When price takes a rapid move in the direction of my trade and then begins to slow down, I watch for a violation of the close of the last two bars in the trend for an exit signal. This is a good way to contain a trend that has moved away from the eight-period SMA or does not lend itself easily to a Fibonacci stop. Once again, the caveat is consolidation. When price starts trading in a tight range at the extreme of a move, I use channel boundaries as stops, since a reversal of two closes will occur simply as a function of price flipping back and forth in the channel.

The kings and queens intraday reversal

This is more of a pattern stop than a stop loss *per se*. This exit triggers when price moves dramatically in our favour in one bar, and then retraces a large portion of that extension in the next. Thus the bar on the left gives us a large additional profit, while the bar to the right takes much of that profit away. I find that this pattern often indicates exhaustion and a potential reversal. When it occurs, I head for the exit.

The 50% scratch stop

Once a position has moved 50% of the distance between my entry and my initial support/resistance target, I move my stop on the trade to just beyond breakeven.

The rules of the game as far as entries and exits go are pretty simple:

1. Enter a trade when the entry price you have planned for ticks. Use a marketable limit order to establish the position. I typically place my buy orders, sell orders, short orders and buy-to-cover orders about .10–.12 beyond the inside quote. This usually results in a fill right around the planned entry price, with the maximum allowable slippage being planned right into the initial order. After that, I do not chase the stock.

2. Set an alert just shy of the stop price and the initial profit target.

3. Sit on your hands and do nothing unless one of your alerts sounds.

4. Exit trades immediately if the predetermined stop price ticks using a marketable limit order.

5. When the trade reaches 50% of the distance between the planned entry price and the initial profit target, trail stops just beyond breakeven.

6. When the initial profit target is met, trail stops to intraday areas of support or resistance immediately. If trading a large share size, take a portion of the open profit.

7. Continue trailing stops as a position moves in your favour. Use intraday support and resistance and/or Fibonacci to establish likely reversal levels.

Summary

The ground rules discussed in this chapter are all about discipline. Developing a disciplined trading methodology is really the only way to get to the point of trading in a non-random, professional manner. Trading is, after all, a business. And no business can survive without a plan.

CHAPTER 4.
Expansion of Range and Volume

WHEN I STARTED my trading career, breakouts on expanded range were so common that all a trader had to do was get up in the morning, buy the continuation move a few pennies above the previous day's high, wait a few minutes and count the money. Unfortunately, those days are over – but breakouts will always be part of trading. The key to capturing profits from breakouts is in identifying which moves are real, and which will be added to the seemingly endless list of failed patterns. The expansion-of-range-and-volume pattern identifies the breakouts that have all the ingredients to fuel a substantial continuation move, while eliminating most of the trades that would unnecessarily churn an account.

The long trade variety of the expansion-of-range-and-volume pattern works best when the day that completes the pattern comes on the heels of a pullback. Another acceptable variation would be a move that emanates from a consolidation in an uptrend.

1. The precursor for pattern formation is a pullback in an uptrend.

2. The stock must break out of the pullback in the direction of the original trend. The move must represent the widest range of the past 10 days, and volume should be higher on the breakout day than the average daily volume during the pullback.

3. On the trigger day, we enter .10 above the high of the breakout bar. Stops should be ratcheted up as soon as the trade is profitable. We close the position by the end of the trading day.

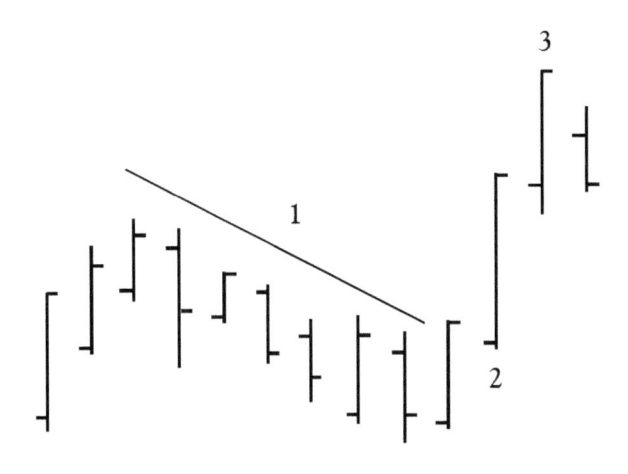

FIGURE 4.1

The alternative set-up involves a consolidation in a trend, and a range expansion move out of the channel in the direction of the underlying move.

The rules for the long trade are as follows:

1. A trending stock must form a 5–15 day consolidation.

2. The stock breaks out of the channel either in the direction of the original trend or counter to the original direction. The move must represent the widest range of the past 10 days, and volume should be higher on the breakout day than the average daily volume during the consolidation.

3. On the trigger day, we enter .10 above the high, or .10 below the low (for shorts) of the breakout bar. Stops should be ratcheted up as soon as the trade is profitable. We close the position by the end of the trading day.

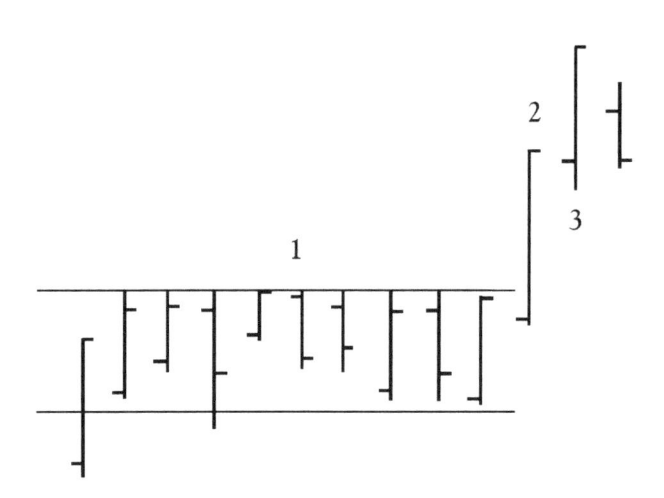

FIGURE 4.2

While the pullback variation of the pattern is taken only in the direction of the dominant trend, the consolidation-type is a trade I will take in either the trend or counter-trend direction. This set-up often triggers when a stock has consolidated and run out of steam, as is illustrated in this example which occurred after Big Lots (BIG) faltered at recent highs and started a slide in July 2012.

1. BIG trades at recent highs and has a violent sell-off and a weak close.

2. The stock forms a seven-day consolidation.

3. Sellers push the stock lower in an expansion-of-range-and-volume move that occurs on heavy volume.

4. The short sale is at $38.79, and the stock immediately trades as low as $38.06 before trailing out on a profit-protecting stop. It is fairly typical to see reversals in the expansion-of-range-and-volume trades after the profit target is achieved. This is one reason I do not ever try to hold a volatility set-up overnight.

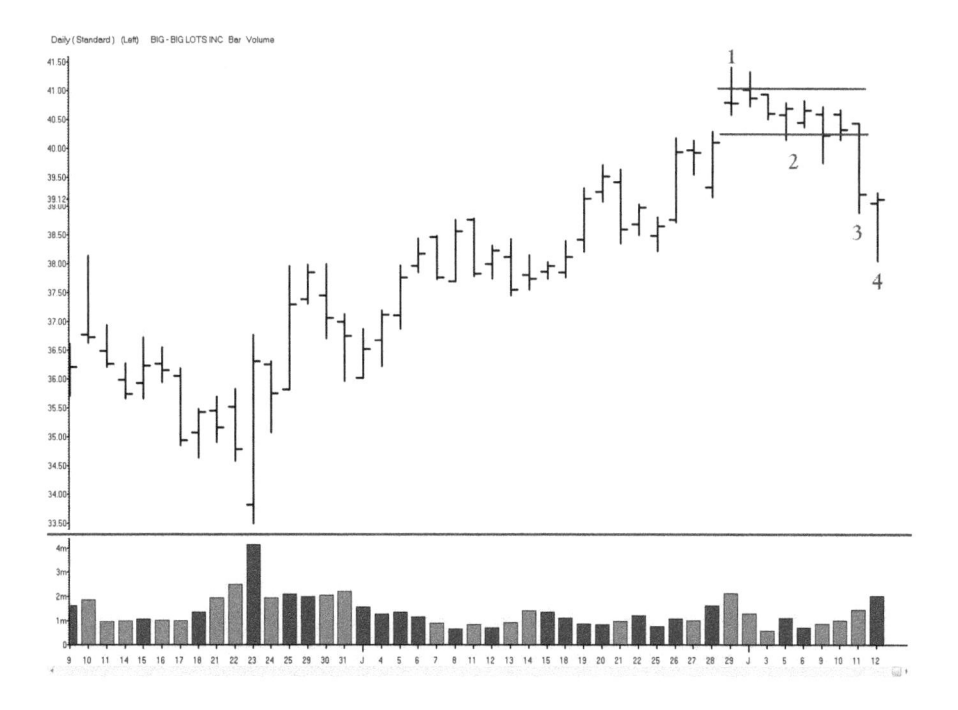

FIGURE 4.3 – BIG LOTS
RealTick® graphics used with permission of RealTick LLC. ©1986-2012 RealTick LLC. All Rights reserved. RealTick® is registered trademark of RealTick LLC.

Energy was as good as gold (better actually) as a trading vehicle in 2012. Many traders shy away from stocks in the energy sectors because they feel that the volatility that characterises their trading poses a threat. But volatility in basic materials presented many good trading opportunities, and when stock in National Fuel Gas (NFG) declined in value by 20% it was a clear indication to me to watch for a panic-driven sell-off in the form of an expansion-of-range-and-volume set-up.

1. A two-week consolidation (A) on the daily chart of NFG yields to a distribution sell-off. The stock loses over $4 per share in a period of five days.

2. A 38.2% Fibonacci retracement terminates with a weak close.

3. The stock has an expansion-of-range-and-volume sell-off on very heavy volume. NFG closes the day at the bottom of its range.

4. A $50.11 entry positions us to realise a $0.57 per-share gain on the trade for the session.

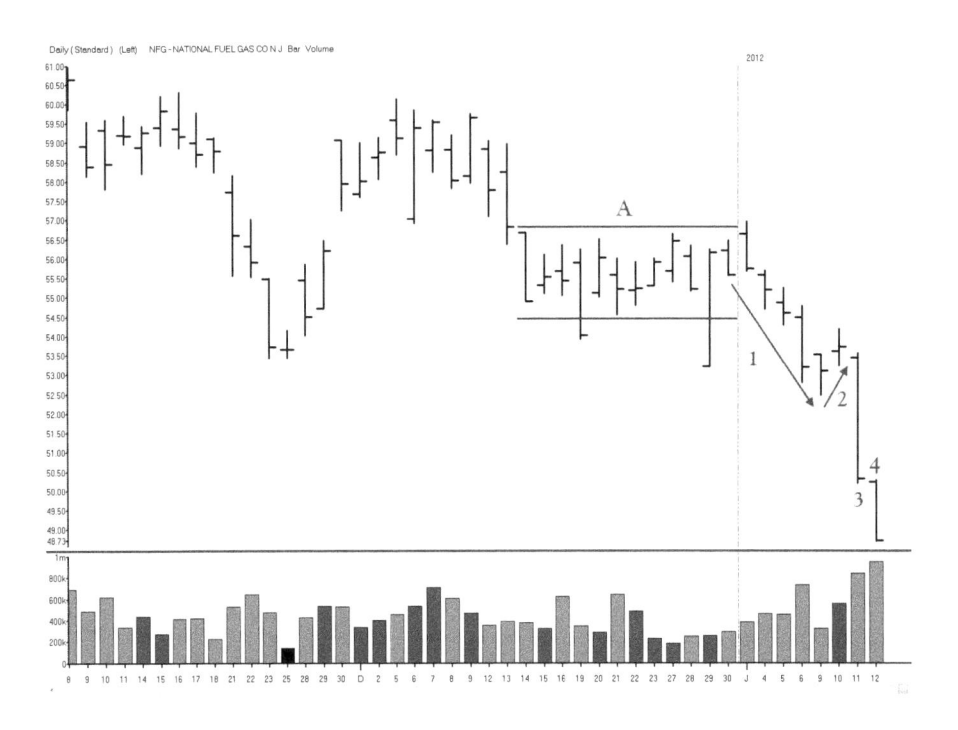

FIGURE 4.4 – NATIONAL FUEL GAS
RealTick by Townsend Analytics, Ltd.

The drillers provide many opportunities to capitalise on expansion-of-range-and-volume set-ups. Many times, multiple set-ups in the energy sector will appear on the same day. As long as the set-ups are clear, I will trade multiple oil and gas signals in the same session. Since volatility in the sector leads to frequent opening gaps after wide-range days, multiple set-ups can serve to get me in front of opportunities.

1. Transoceanic Limited (RIG) lost 11 points in the first three weeks of May 2012. The stock then formed a two-week consolidation.

2. An expansion-of-range-and-volume move to the downside sets up a short sale trading opportunity.

3. On the trigger day, the stock opens flat and attempts to rally. Buying is met with immediate supply, and an entry triggers 10 minutes into the session. We net $0.52 per share in the first half hour of the trading day.

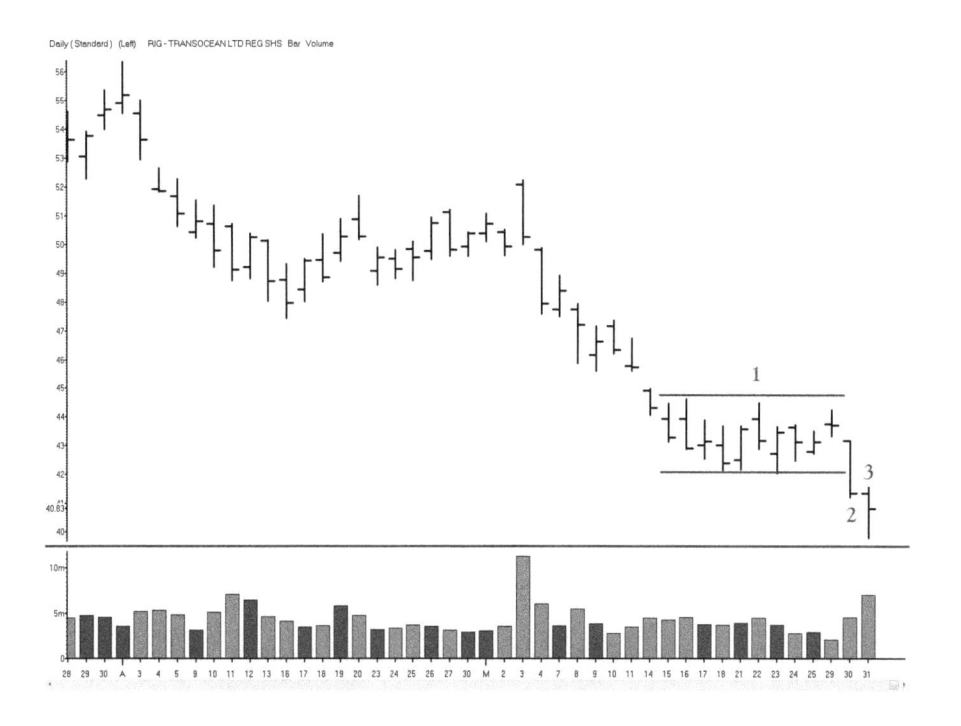

FIGURE 4.5 – TRANSOCEANIC LIMITED
RealTick by Townsend Analytics, Ltd.

Another oil and gas set-up occurred the same day as the consolidate-and-expand trade in RIG. This time it was Canadian Natural Resources (CNQ), a pullback-and-expand set-up. These two different set-ups in the same sector gave me extra confidence that the sector was going to lose ground during the coming session.

1. A major sell-off in CNQ moves the stock to its 2012 low after the company announces first quarter earnings of $0.27 per share versus consensus estimates of $0.47.

2. A 50% Fibonacci retracement of the A–B decline moves the stock to resistance (C) encountered earlier in the month.

3. A gap open forms an expansion-of-range-and-volume sell-off on very heavy volume.

4. CNQ opens for trading and attempts to rally. The stock meets supply and the sell-off continues. The stock trades smoothly to the profit target in the first few hours of trading.

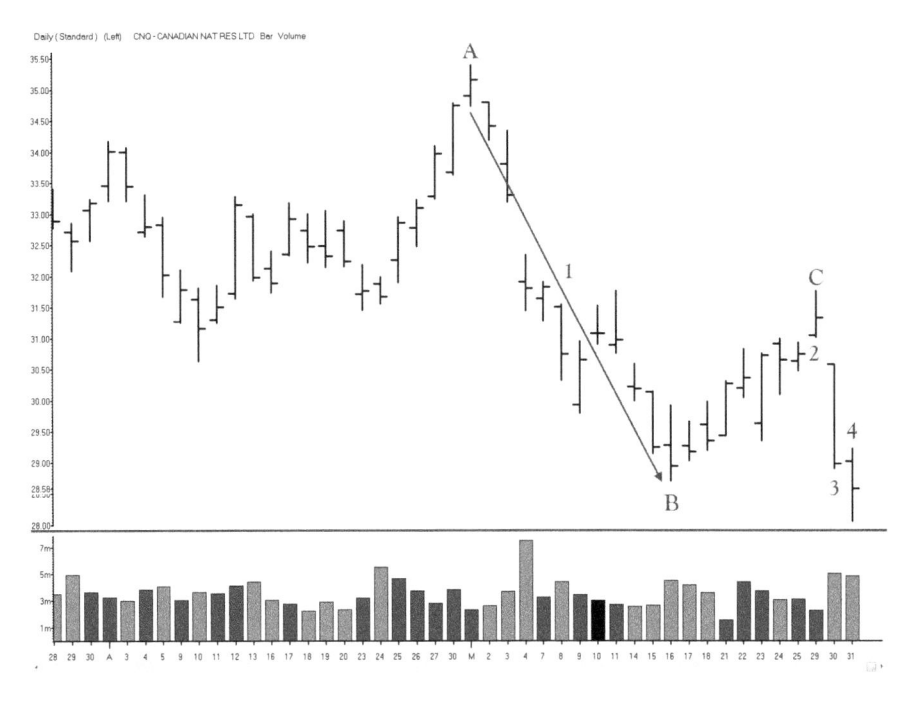

FIGURE 4.6 – CANADIAN NATURAL RESOURCES
RealTick by Townsend Analytics, Ltd.

High level short-side set-ups make for some of my favourite trades. When a stock trades sharply higher over a few days or weeks, and then shows signs of meeting overhead supply, it is usually a good indication that accumulation will soon end as buyers will no longer be forced to chase prices higher. When the buying pressure vanishes, the most recent owners of a stock are usually the first ones to head for the exit. This can create expansion-of-range-and-volume implosions that can unravel recent price appreciation very quickly. A set-up in Community Health Systems (CYH) provides a good example.

1. A gap-expansion move in CYH propels the stock higher after a Wells Fargo upgrade.

2. Overhead supply is met at the level that created a previous 52-week high in 2011. The stock begins to retrace some of its recent gains.

3. A shallow low-volume pullback toward recent highs fails to gain momentum.

4. An expansion-of-range-and-volume bar sets up a short sale at $22.90 with a target at $22.37 support.

5. CYH trades exactly to the target, yielding a $0.53 per share gain. The stock bounces higher later in the session, but there is no opportunity for a second entry.

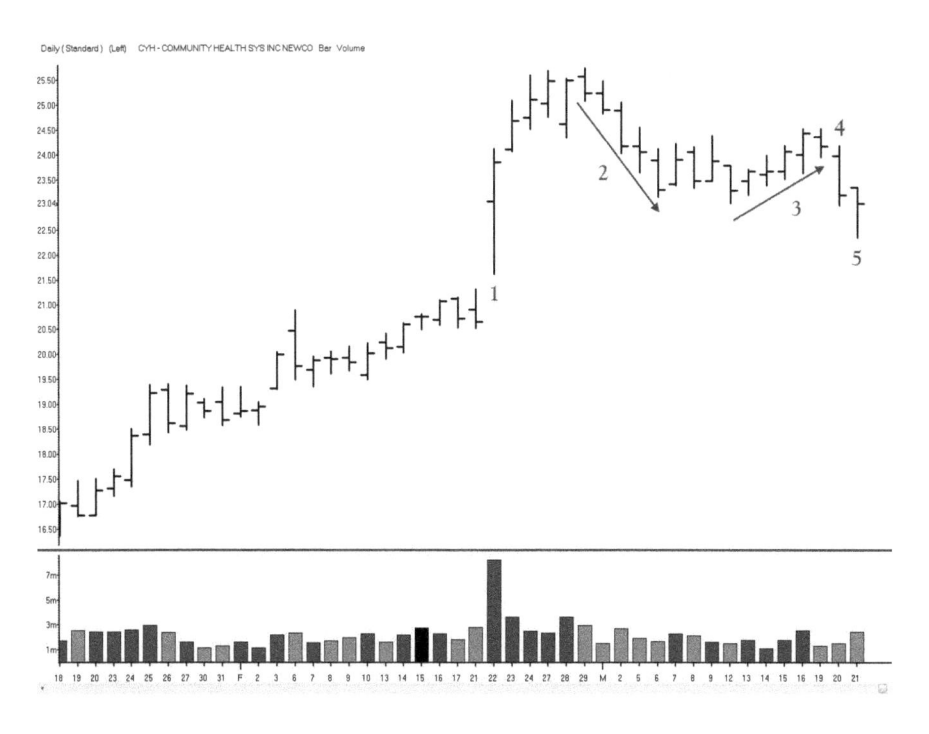

FIGURE 4.7 – COMMUNITY HEALTH SYSTEMS
RealTick by Townsend Analytics, Ltd.

The expansion-of-range-and-volume set-up had a heavy bias toward the short side of the market in 2012. But that does not preclude planning trades for long entries when the opportunity presents itself. BRE Properties Inc. (BRE) is just one of many examples on the buy side, and it illustrates the primary drawback of long trades in a market that is climbing back from a recent significant move lower. Namely, profit targets will be much narrower than they are when selling short because overhead supply exerts itself much more forcefully as a stock climbs out of a trench than demand does during a move lower. Stocks typically drop much faster than they rise.

1. BRE has a gap-and-go breakaway and begins to move higher.

2. May 2012 resistance is encountered and the stock pulls back.

3. An expansion-of-range-and-volume move to the upside sets up a trade with an entry at $52.05 and a target at $52.44 overhead resistance.

4. The stock trades through our profit target and makes a slight extension move higher.

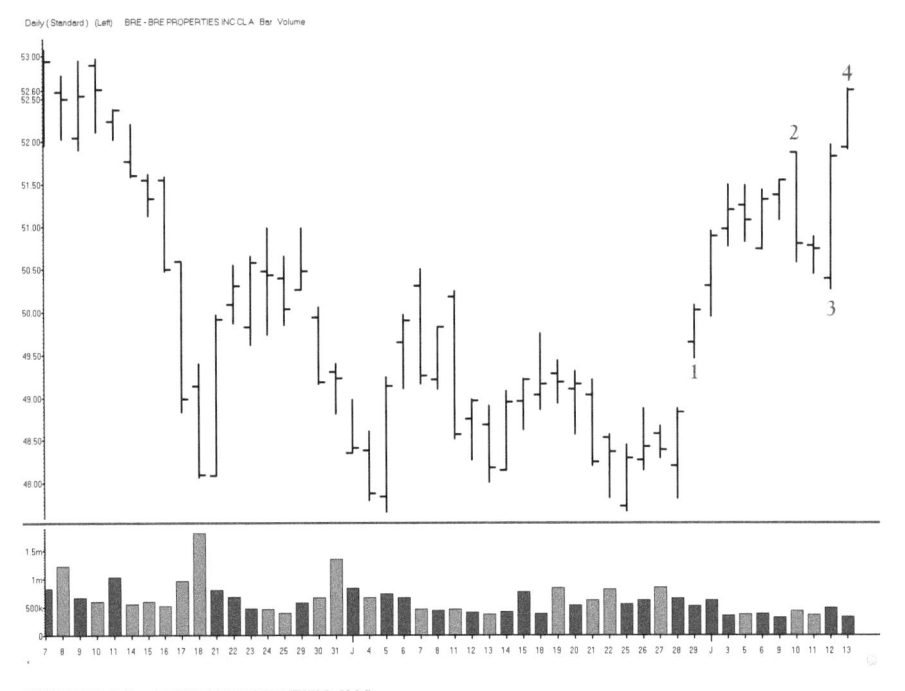

FIGURE 4.8 – BRE PROPERTIES INC.
RealTick by Townsend Analytics, Ltd.

Summary

The expansion-of-range-and-volume pattern works because it relies on pent-up energy to cause momentum to reassert itself. This makes it a much more conservative approach to trading breakouts than simply entering the continuation of every wide range bar the market hands us. This means that we miss quite a few breakouts to new highs, but with so many range expansions failing I really don't mind being rained out sometimes. I like this pattern as much for what it avoids as for the opportunities it presents. When the pattern comes together just right, the expansion-of-range-and-volume is a consistent, reliable and conservative approach to riding a quick and profitable move.

CHAPTER 5.
Extension Reversals

OFTEN TIMES, STRONGLY trending stocks will move too far too fast, making a pullback a foregone conclusion. A reaction open can take a stock much higher than is warranted. The result can be an immediate sell-off or a steady drift back toward the previous day's high. When gap openings are followed by poor intraday price support, the stage is set for a move that will fill the void. Spotting these opportunities and knowing how to capitalise on them is one of the best ways to take money from the market. The key is to find moves in stocks that are showing all the signs of exhaustion. Trading the extension-reversal pattern correctly has proven to be my most predictable and most profitable intraday technique. This is a short-only strategy, making for clear, unambiguous entries and exits. The extension reversal is a bread-and-butter trade that will test a speculator's short-selling skills and provide handsome rewards when follow-through comes our way. While overall market conditions can push the trade toward the desired outcome, a broader move lower is not necessary for success.

The extension reversal relies on the fear factor to generate profits. Basically, we are looking for stocks to move sharply to the upside and to be pushed too far in too short a time frame. This set-up relies on a gap day to take a price higher but fail to put in a strong close. The next session, we look for a short-selling opportunity and a move to profits.

The entry criteria for the short sale are as follows:

1. A move up on a daily chart culminates with a gap higher which closes in the lower half of its range. Ideally, there is room for profit between the low of the gap day and the high of the previous day, but the pattern works very well even if there is not.

2. The stock must break the low of the gap day by at least .10 to trigger an entry. If the position closes strongly in our favour we will carry a 30–50% portion overnight.

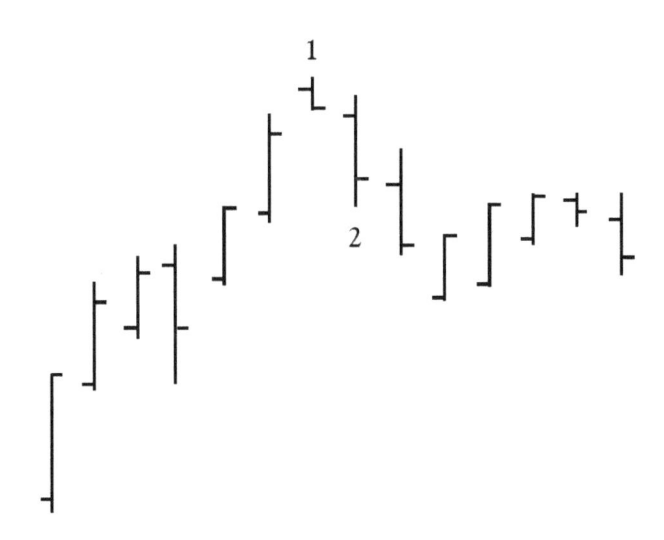

FIGURE 5.1

Recent gap attempts can often lend insight into the probable behaviour of a stock if it is gapped again. In the case of Symbol Companhia De Bebidas (ABV), an American depositary receipt (ADR) that we frequently trade, there are numerous recent gaps that provide indication of what may happen if the stock is gapped again.

When the stock gapped and had reversal days multiple times in late 2011 and early 2012, we anticipated an opportunity for a good trade and looked for extension-reversal set-ups every time ABV made a move higher.

1. ABV makes multiple extension-reversal moves over the course of five weeks of trading.

2. An extension-reversal set-up presents itself on the daily chart but does not trigger the following session.

3. Another gap higher closes poorly and provides us with a planned entry for the next session.

4. The stock opens and immediately triggers a short sale. We lock in $0.42 per share in profits, exiting at the initial profit target for the position.

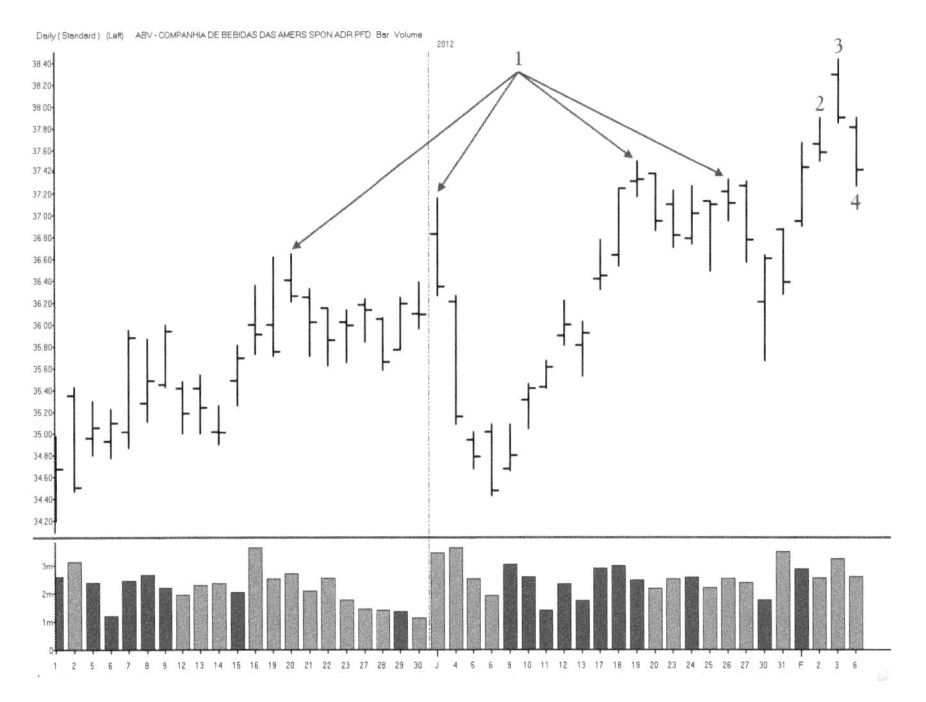

FIGURE 5.2 – SYMBOL COMPANHIA DE BEBIDAS
RealTick by Townsend Analytics, Ltd.

38 | Beat the Street

I trade quite a few retail stocks, and Gap Inc. (GPS) is one of the more volatile set-ups when it presents itself. The stock typically has good intraday moves and fits into the volatility parameters that I like to trade. When set-ups occur in this one they generally have good follow-through and significant intraday travel range.

1. GPS made a trending move higher as unseasonably warm weather boosted February sales significantly. This – combined with a positive news piece, a 2% yield and a 24% return on equity – had the stock moving higher nearly every day.

2. A news-driven gap higher attempted to rally, but ended the trading session in the bottom of the day's range. I planned an extension-reversal entry .10 below the low of the session with a $24.33 initial target.

3. The stock opened and tried to rally again. An entry trigger was followed by smooth trading lower and an exit at the session close at $24.43, just shy of the natural support target.

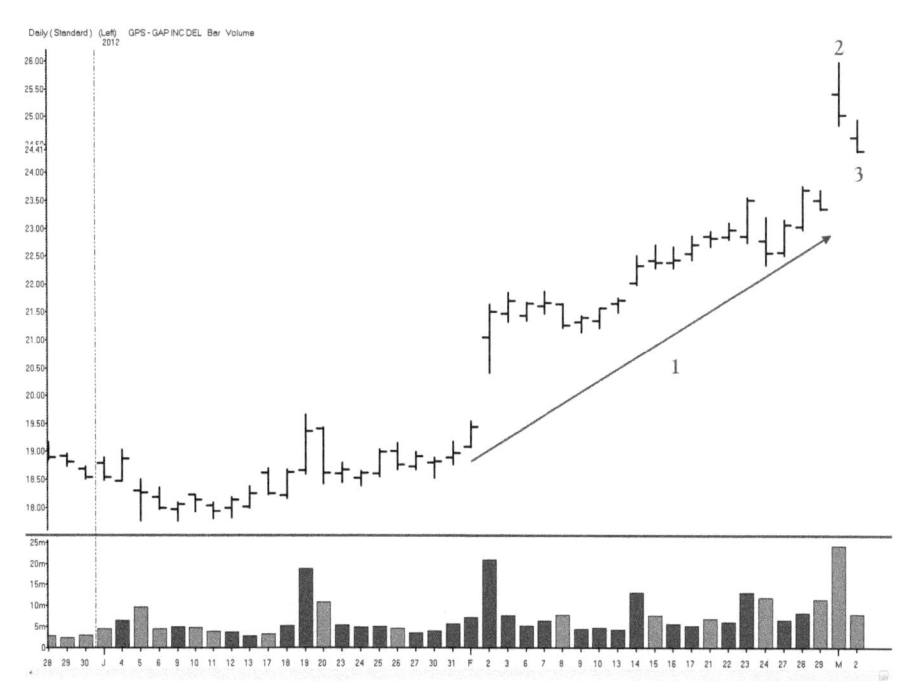

FIGURE 5.3 – GAP INC.
RealTick by Townsend Analytics, Ltd.

A chart pattern does not need to be picture-perfect to be a candidate for my trading. As long as a day's trading activity is in the spirit of one of my set-ups, I will work through the numbers and assess the viability of the trade. Valeant Pharmaceuticals (VRX) is a stock I frequently work with. I find the intraday trading behavior of VRX to be fairly predictable, and when this less-than-perfect extension-reversal appeared in the first quarter of 2012 I was eager to capitalise on the opportunity.

1. VRX makes a 10-day move higher and adds 20% to its valuation in the process. Rumours are circulating that the company will, once again, attempt to take over biotech company Cephalon (CEPH).

2. The stock puts in a swing high on decreasing volume. The resulting extension-reversal set-up is imperfect as it closed above its opening price, but the intraday price activity indicates weakening demand and a short-sale opportunity.

3. VRX gaps past the planned entry in the morning and attempts to rally higher. A test of the extension-reversal day's closing range fails, and the stock trades lower through the trigger price, posting a $0.60 per share profit on the session.

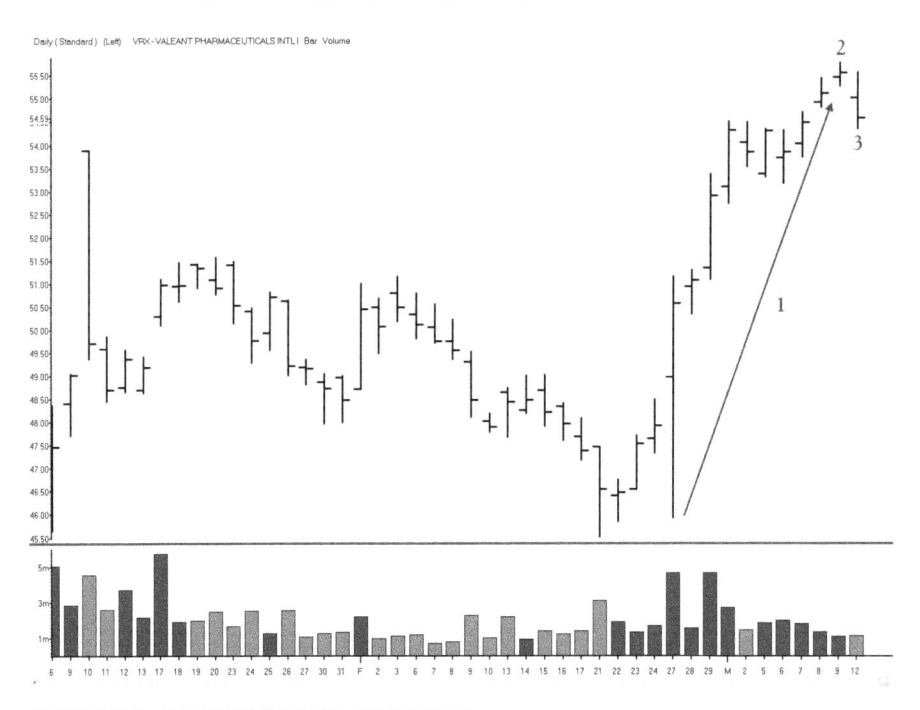

FIGURE 5.4 – VALEANT PHARMACEUTICALS
RealTick by Townsend Analytics, Ltd.

Flexible thinking is as an important characteristic for any trader who hopes to achieve success. This applies to finding opportunities and to capitalising on them. When Ashland Inc. (ASH) made a big move higher and then left an extension-reversal bar on the daily chart, the trigger day appeared to have little profit opportunity because the stock gapped past the planned entry. But persistence and patience are frequently rewarded in trading, and ASH still managed to hand over profits before the day was over.

1. ASH makes a two-week move higher. The stock makes frequent large constructive moves with predictable mean-reverting retracements. When the directional move is evident, I start watching for the signs of a reversal in the making. When the 17 April 2012 gap extension led to an inside day on 18 April, the stock looked poised to make a reversal move lower sometime soon.

2. An extension-reversal day closes in the bottom of its range. The profit target for the set-up is at $63.36, in the upper support and resistance zone of the 17 April and 18 April intraday trading sessions.

3. The stock gaps lower and spends much of the day stuck in a trading range. Late in the session, ASH trades higher than the planned entry price by the $0.08 threshold that I require, and reverses lower triggering an entry. There is insufficient time to travel all of the distance to the target, but by the close we book $0.28 per share in profits.

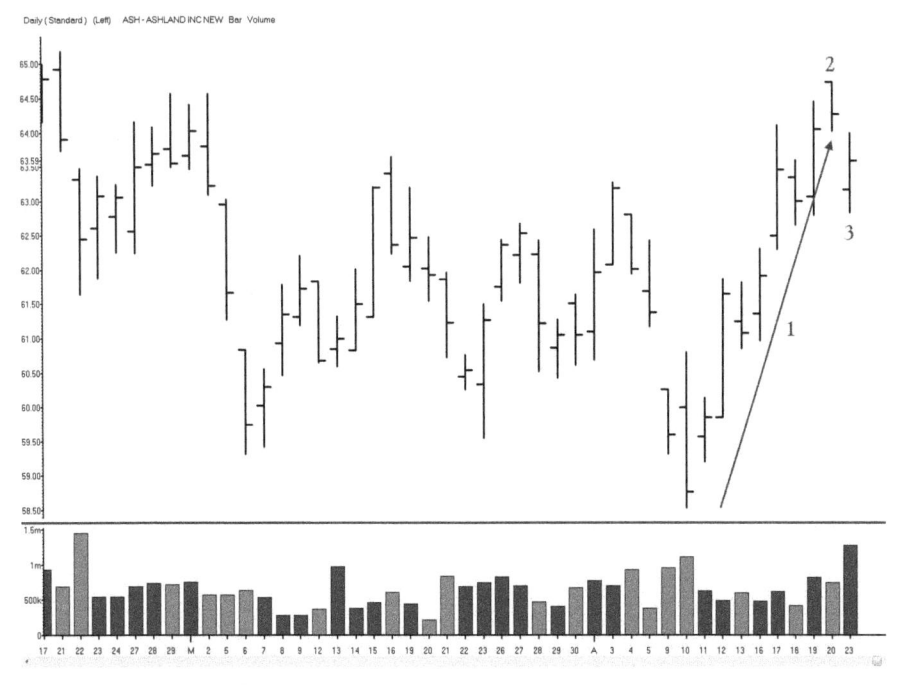

FIGURE 5.5 – ASHLAND INC.
RealTick by Townsend Analytics, Ltd.

5. Extension Reversals | **41**

Omnicom Group (OMC) is a stock that appears on my trading plan on a regular basis. OMC makes frequent orderly trending moves, and when it gets extended the reversal swings tend to provide good profits. The year 2012 saw the stock in a solid year-long move that provided many good set-ups.

1. A trend continuation move gains ground for three consecutive weeks. OMC reaches four-year highs when General Motors announces that an Omnicom company will become the global ad agency for Chevrolet.

2. An extension-reversal set-up forms on heavy sell-side volume.

3. On the trigger day, the OMC short sale posts a $0.60 per-share gain.

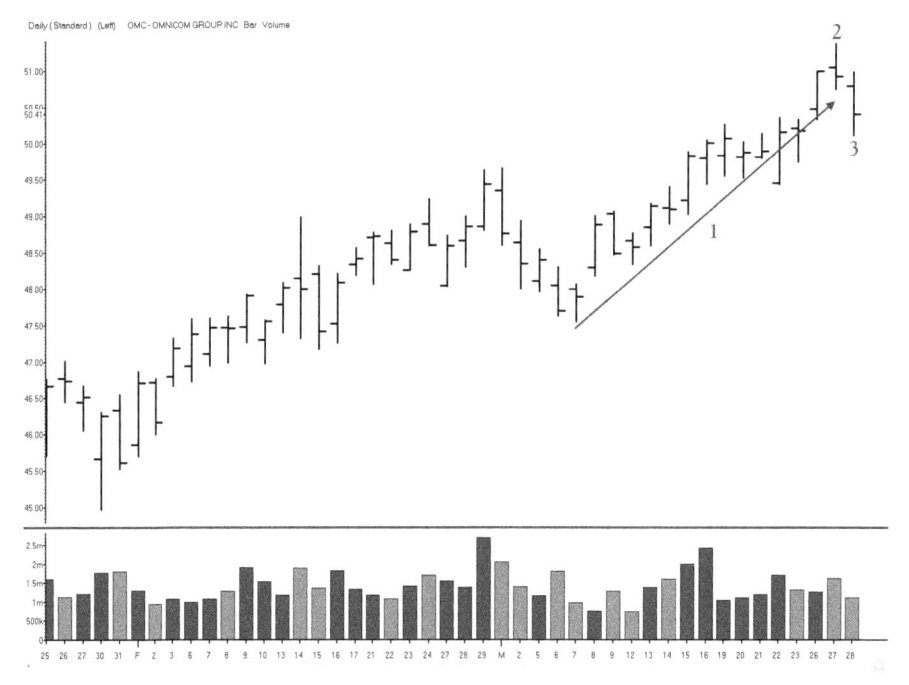

FIGURE 5.6 – OMNICOM
RealTick by Townsend Analytics, Ltd.

Abbott Labs (ABT) is one of the big movers on the NYSE. The stock has many mean-reverting moves after price extensions, and this makes it a great candidate for extension reversals.

1. A thrust to the upside on extremely heavy volume has ABT trading at all-time highs.

2. The stock attempts to push higher again, but volume is comparatively low, and the close is in the bottom of the range. The extension-reversal entry is planned .10 below the low of the day.

3. A gap lower reverses and qualifies the stock for a trade later in the session. The stock trades smoothly to the support target at $64.97.

FIGURE 5.7 – ABBOTT LABS
RealTick by Townsend Analytics, Ltd.

Summary

Like most things in life, if a stock move looks too good to be true, it probably is. The extension reversal is a powerful pattern that allows you to capitalise on the irrational exuberance that propels stocks higher, without having to play the guessing game of picking tops. If the pattern triggers, it usually does so definitively. There is no time to second-guess entries, as shorting fast movers can be tricky business. Determine the maximum amount of slippage you are willing to accept and price it into the trade before pulling the trigger. I find that aiming a little lower with these moves provides more opportunity for a fill at an improved price, while lessening the likelihood of the move leaving us behind.

CHAPTER 6. Gap Extensions

THERE IS MUCH by way of 'conventional wisdom' regarding reaction moves the day after a breakaway gap. Many traders avoid any position in the direction of the gap, feeling that price action will be choppy and that there is a virtual certainty that the void will fill in over the course of hours or days. Traders will frequently attempt to fade the move in the hope of catching the contra-extension for a profit. The gap-extension pattern seeks to capitalise on those instances in which these individuals are wrong and price continues to advance or decline in the direction of the gap. When this pattern works, it generally hands over quick profits. When it fails, it usually either does not trigger or results in a small loss. These characteristics make it a good intraday trade. I generally close this position at the end of the session. The fact is, many gaps do fill, and the object of the trade is to capture the quick profit, not a multiday-continuation move. This is a long pattern only. I do not use the gap extension for shorts.

The set-up for the long trade is as follows:

1. Today the stock must form a breakaway gap, making a 10-day high. The close must be above the open and in the top 25% of the bar.

2. Tomorrow, we will take a position .10 to .12 cents above the high of the breakaway bar.

3. Trail stops .05 to .10 under intraday support of the breakaway day or .05 to .10 under the trade day pivot or support 1.

4. The initial profit target is approximately at the resistance 1 level.

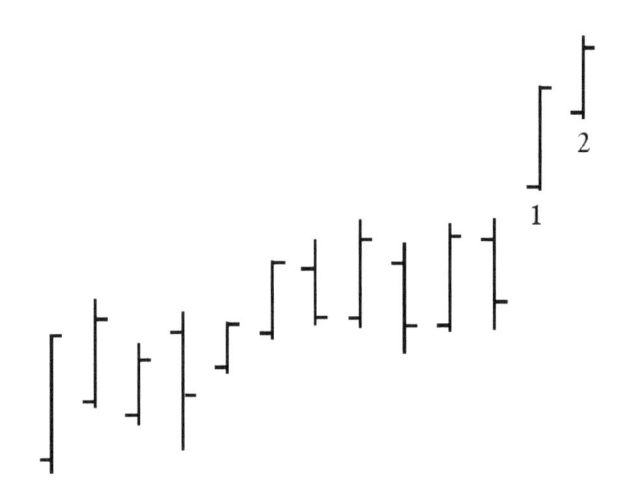

FIGURE 6.1

I actively search for set-ups that occur in cyclical sequence. Stocks move through periods of accumulation, mark-up, distribution, and mark-down. If I can find pattern entries that occur in a predictable portion of that cycle, then the outcome of the potential trade will usually be easier to predict than an entry based on a pattern that presents itself as an outlier. When a ratio pullback is followed by a gap extension, the set-up usually has enough pent-up demand to get to the next level of overhead supply very quickly. Ensco PLC (ESV), in the volatile oil and gas sector, provides a nice example of what I like to see for this set-up.

1. A ratio pullback after a distribution and mark-down have led to renewed interest in the stock.

2. A gap extension bar on the daily chart has ESV on my trading plan for the following day.

3. ESV triggers and trades to the support/resistance target for the session.

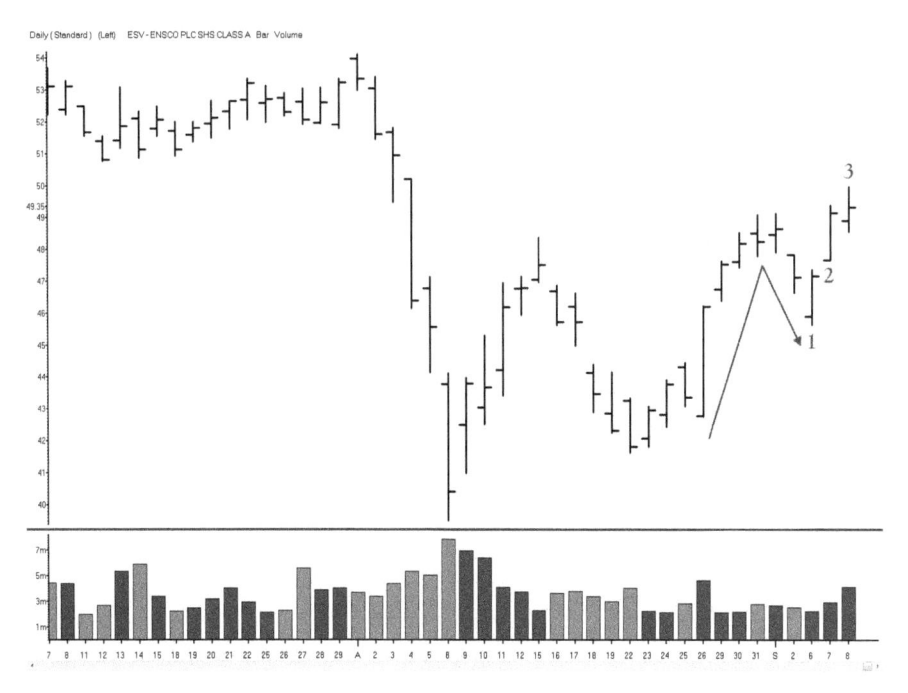

FIGURE 6.2 – ENSCO PLC
RealTick by Townsend Analytics, Ltd.

6. Gap Extensions | 47

Health Care REIT Inc. (HCN) sold off after placing a secondary offering of 18 million shares in February 2012. The stock then spent several months in an accumulation phase and started a mark-up phase with a gap extension move out of the accumulation range. These 'low level' set-ups often make for fast profits as sidelined bargain hunters enter the market in search of a big move.

1. A gap extension out of the three-month accumulation range occurs. My planned entry on the trade is $56.09, .10 above the high of the 26 April bar.

2. A soft open and a dip initially send HCN lower but, later in the session, the stock triggers and makes a swift move to the $56.75 profit target.

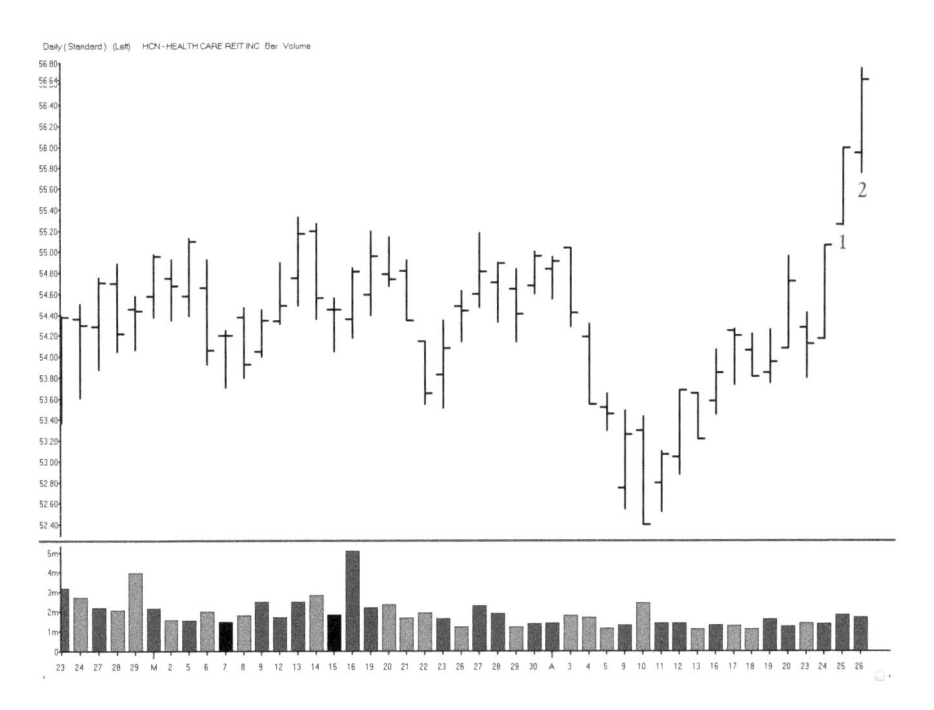

FIGURE 6.3 – HEALTH CARE REIT INC.
RealTick by Townsend Analytics, Ltd.

Potash producers Mosaic (MOS) and Potash (POT) are some of my favorite intraday trading vehicles. They have large intraday trading ranges, and tend to follow through when they start moving. In this example, MOS makes a gap extension after a profitable ratio-pullback set-up.

1. MOS retraces 38.2% of its recent move higher.

2. A gap extension occurs after the price of new corn was reported up 2% to its highest level since November 2011. A government report indicated that corn crops had greater-than-expected damage, and this moves MOS, a fertiliser producer, over the recent swing high. The stock finds end-of-day support above the apex of the recent move.

3. The stock opens and trades through the planned trigger. A trip to the initial profit target is followed by a move to the lows of the session. Once again, sticking to the plan and taking profits at logical support pays off.

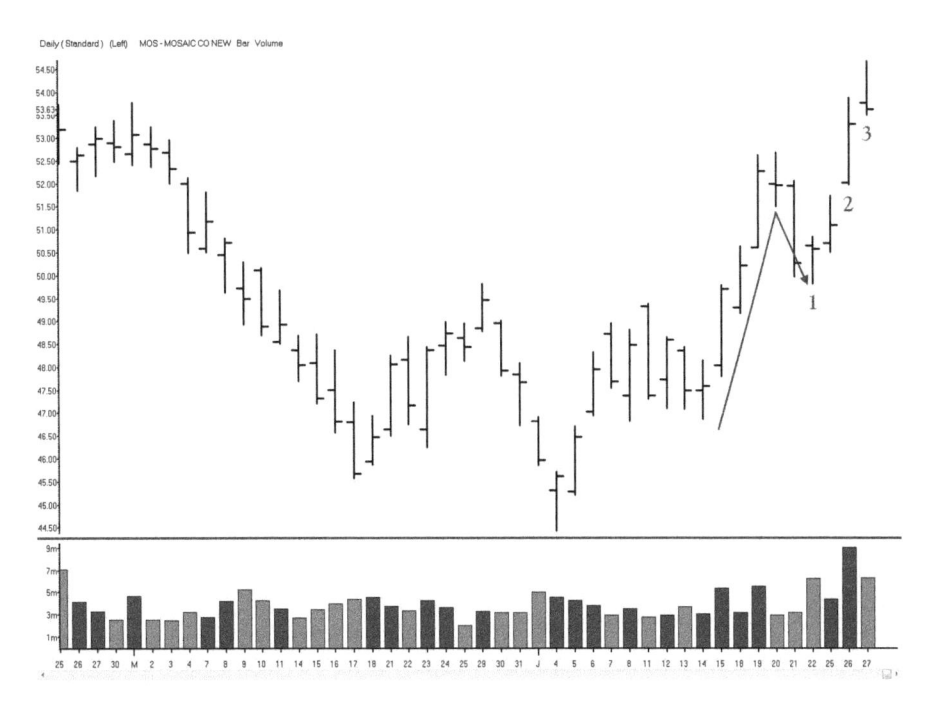

FIGURE 6.4 – MOSAIC
RealTick by Townsend Analytics, Ltd.

Analyst upgrades can give a stock a short-term push higher. When a gap extension sets up after an upgrade there is frequently room to profit. In the example in Figure 6.5 we see the effects of such an upgrade on shares of retailer Big Lots (BIG).

1. BIG is trading in a secondary accumulation range going into the end of 2011.

2. Wedbush upgrades the stock and BIG makes a gap extension higher. An entry is planned for the following session at .10 above the high of the gap extension daily bar.

3. BIG gaps higher again, then trades down below the planned entry price, moves higher, triggers an entry, and closes trading just below our initial profit target.

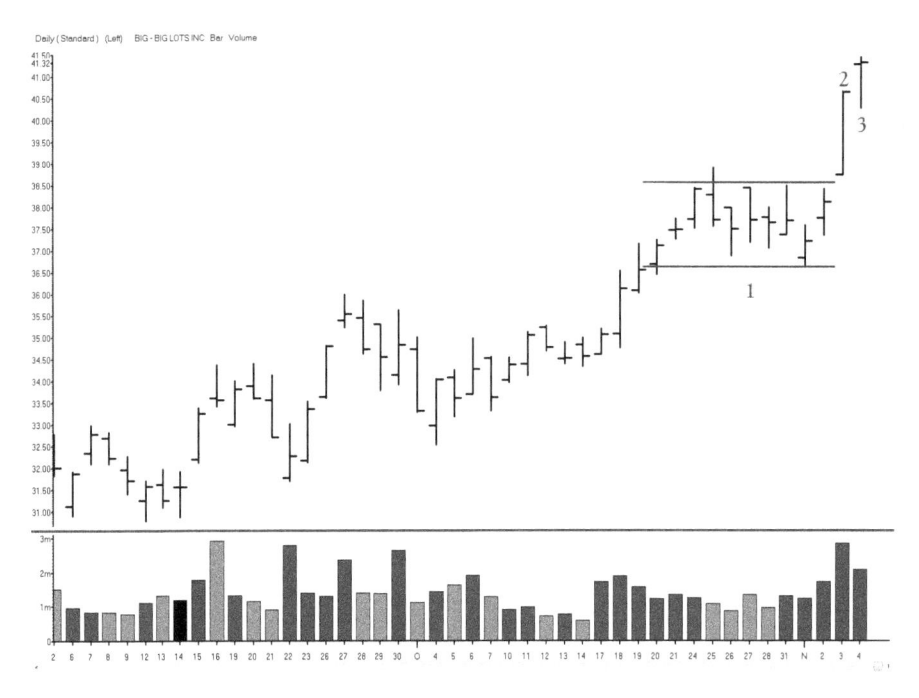

FIGURE 6.5 – BIG LOTS
RealTick by Townsend Analytics, Ltd.

American depositary receipts (ADRs) can make for some difficult trading. ADRs were introduced to the American exchanges as a means of trading shares of foreign companies in the 1920s. The shares are purchased by banks and bundled for sale in the US. This results in increased volatility between closes and opens, as trading activity in the rest of the world during the overnight American session can cause gaps on the daily ADR charts. Many of these gaps wind up reversing, so planned trades have a tendency not to trigger unless they occur against an ideal backdrop.

1. A long, wide consolidation range in shares of Companhia de Bebidas das Americas (ABV). This is one of the most liquid ADRs trading on the NYSE, and gap moves tend to follow through to channel support and resistance.

2. The stock forms a gap extension set-up and closes above its 50-period simple moving average.

3. ABV opens and immediately trades through our entry price. By the end of the session a $1.50 per-share gain is achieved.

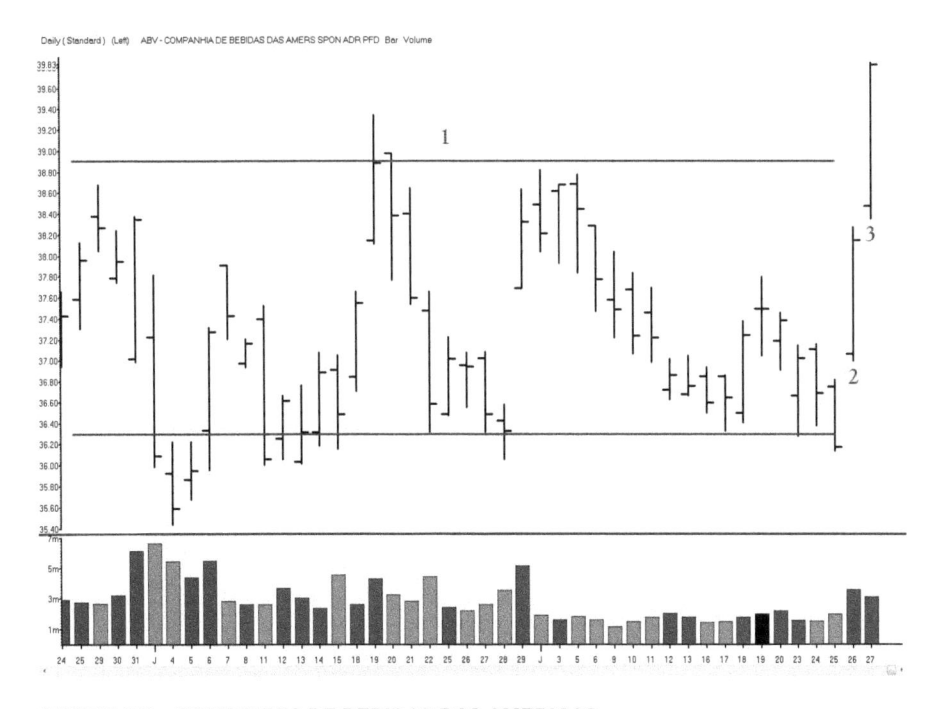

FIGURE 6.6 – COMPANHIA DE BEBIDAS DAS AMERICAS
RealTick by Townsend Analytics, Ltd.

6. Gap Extensions | 51

The markets were expecting good things from Moody's Corp. (MCO) when it was to report earnings before the open of trading on 26 July 2012. The company did not disappoint the analysts, achieving earnings per share (EPS) of $0.76 and quarterly revenue of $640 billion. Both numbers beat the street's consensus, and this sent the stock soaring on the session.

1. MCO gaps higher after releasing its quarterly earnings and revenues. We plan an entry at $40.49 with an initial profit target at $40.99, which represents daily overhead resistance.

2. The stock opens flat, triggers the entry and moves swiftly to the profit target.

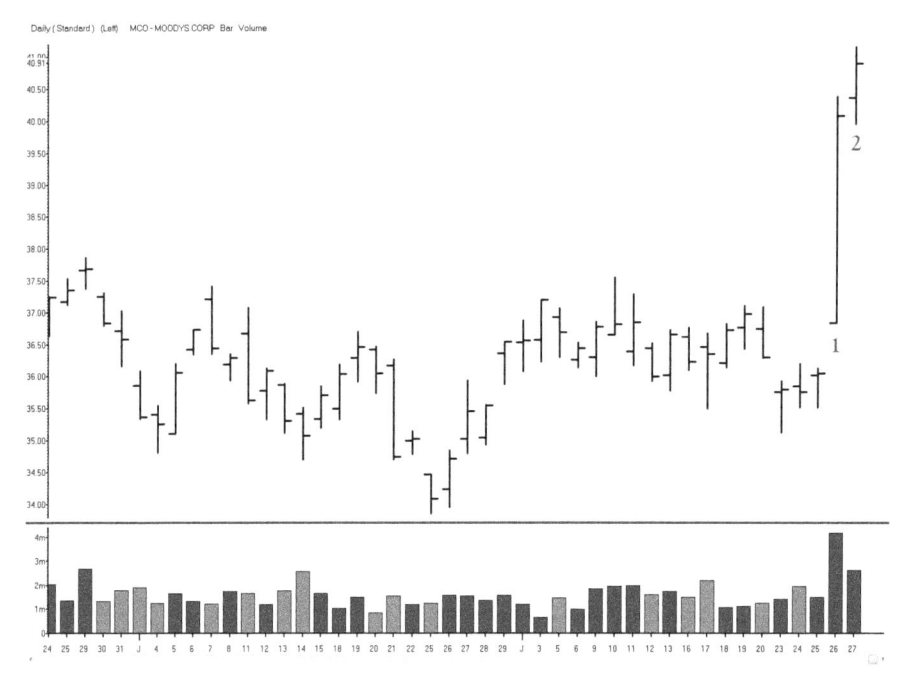

FIGURE 6.7 – MOODY'S CORP.
RealTick by Townsend Analytics, Ltd.

Summary

The gap extension is a simple pattern that works well when a stock, its underlying sector and the market are trending. It capitalises on the ability of a security to gap open and hold its gains without immediately filling the void between the current session low and the previous day's trading range. With the markets volatile, I use this pattern strictly as a day trade; but if a strong upward trend exerts itself, the gap extension can set up some nice swing positions.

CHAPTER 7. Expansion-of-Range Reversals

MAKE-OR-BREAK SET-UPS don't come along that often, and when they do, they are rarely worth the effort involved in finding them. The expansion-of-range reversal is an exception to the rule. This one takes days to form, and many potential set-ups never trigger. When an expansion-of-range reversal does trigger an entry, it can make for a profitable intraday or swing trade with a good risk/reward ratio. The pattern relies on market participants to push a trending stock rapidly higher and then sell it off for profits. Then, when all the gains of the upward thrust seem to be in danger of turning into losses, the strong money enters the market and drives the stock higher again. When the move plays out, we hold a portion overnight as a swing trade.

Often traders drive price higher on good volume and with an expanded trading range. These are the ingredients that create the expansion-of-range-and-volume set-up. Unfortunately for breakout traders, profits must often be taken quickly on these moves as they are much more prone to failure than they were in the runaway bull market of the past. The expansion-of-range reversals pattern uses a pattern failure and a subsequent pullback as the primary ingredients for a long set-up that can lead to substantial profits.

Here are the rules for buys (short sales are reversed):

1. An expansion-of-range-and-volume break.

2. The trigger either does not happen or results in a loss.

3. The stock has a one-to-five day pullback.

4. We enter on an intraday breakout of the high of the deepest pullback bar.

5. A portion of any profitable position may be carried over as a swing trade.

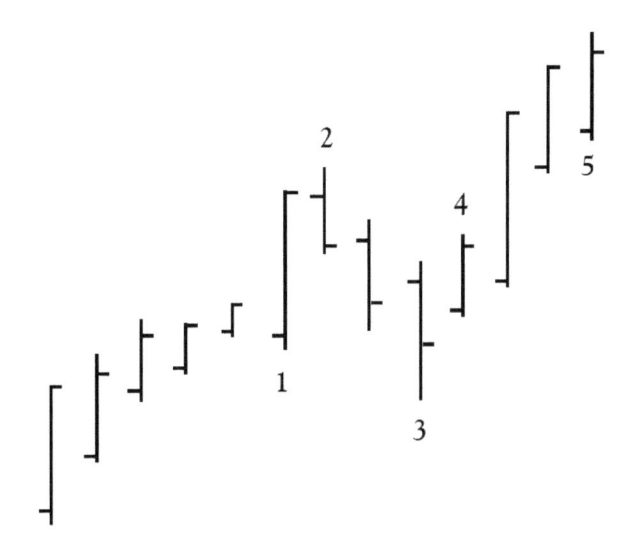

FIGURE 7.1

Anglogold Ashanti Ltd (AU) is an ADR that I like very much as a proxy for gold. It has good intraday travel range and the bid-ask spreads are generally very tight. AU has experienced a one-year slide in its share price, and short-side continuation set-ups are generally what I focus on right now in the stock.

In this example, we see the potential that failed set-ups have if a trader stays with the stock and sector bias and keeps looking for the opportunity that an expansion of range and volume signals.

1. An expansion of range and volume breaks through support and occurs on the heels of a ratio pullback (A–B–C) that also forms a kings-and-queens set-up (C).

2. A failed breakdown leaves us with a breakeven stop on the expansion-of-range-and-volume follow-through day.

3. An expansion-of-range reversal occurs. The planned entry is a short sale at $36.37, .10 below the reversal bar, and .02 below the expansion-of-range-and-volume bar. If the price were not below this level, I would require that an opportunity for profit exists between the low of the bar labeled 3 in Figure 7.2 and the low of the bar labelled 1.

4. AU breaks through support for a $0.71-per-share move during the session.

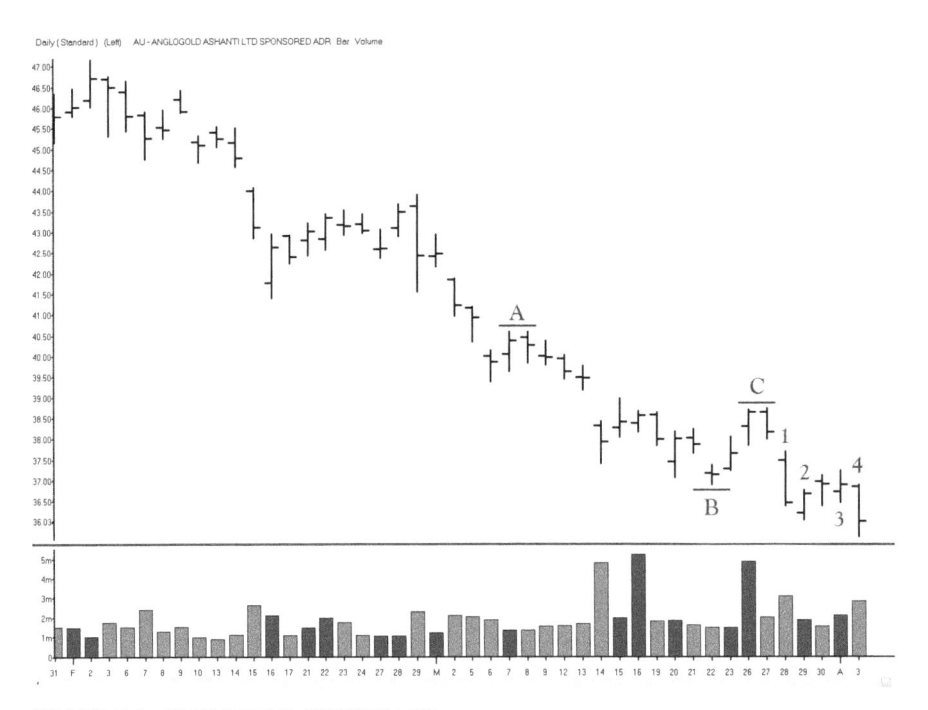

FIGURE 7.2 – ANGLOGOLD ASHANTI LTD
RealTick by Townsend Analytics, Ltd.

Very large expansion-of-range-and-volume moves are frequently followed by inside days, as a stock consolidates gains or losses and traders come to agree on a new value zone. In the case of Archer Daniels Midland Co. (ADM), the expansion-day move was on quadruple average volume and range, and the reversal represented a 50% retracement. I always feel that multiple signals in the same direction increase the probability of a profitable trade.

1. ADM makes an expansion-of-range-and-volume move and closes in the top 10% of its range. The company restated third quarter results to reflect EPS of $0.78. Previous results were reported at $0.59 per share. Additional fuel was added to the stock's gains by news that demand for corn was significantly higher than expected and that cost restructuring would save ADM $150 million.

2. After failing to break higher, the stock retraces 50% of the expansion-day range and leaves an expansion-of-range-reversal set-up.

3. On the trigger day, ADM misses its target but still manages to book a $0.30-per-share profit on the session.

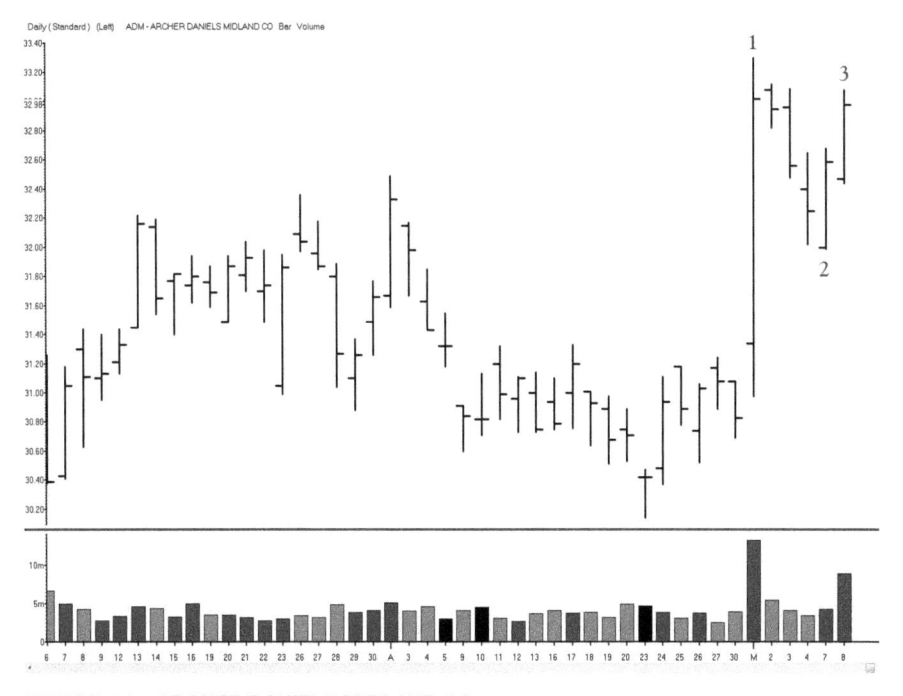

FIGURE 7.3 – ARCHER DANIELS MIDLAND CO.
RealTick by Townsend Analytics, Ltd.

In years past there has not been as much overlap between patterns as there was in 2012. In the case of Baxter Pharmaceuticals in Figure 7.4, an expansion-of-range-and-volume set-up is also a gap extension, and the follow-up expansion-of-range-reversal set-up also qualifies as an expansion consolidation.

1. An expansion-of-range-and-volume bar is also a gap extension.

2. The inside days form an expansion consolidation and a shallow pullback in the form of a symmetrical triangle. The entry is planned .10 above the bar labelled 2.

3. A $59.22 entry yields $0.50 per share in profits.

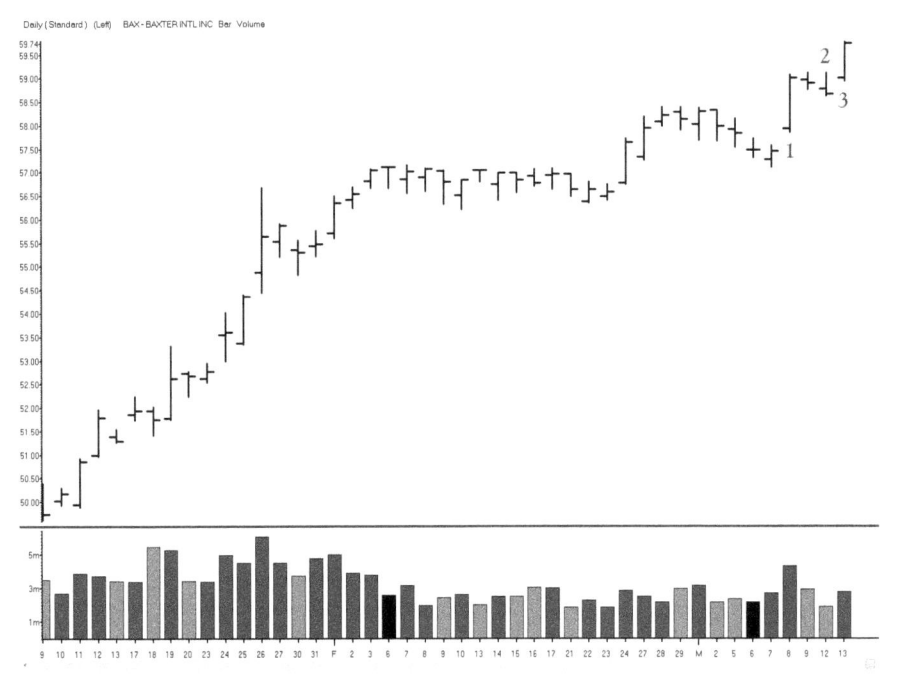

FIGURE 7.4 – BAXTER PHARMACEUTICALS
RealTick by Townsend Analytics, Ltd.

Celanese Corp. (CE) is a textbook example of an expansion-of-range-reversal set-up. The stock traded higher on accelerating momentum and left a non-ratio pullback before thrusting higher and retesting resistance.

1. An expansion-of-range-and-volume day closes off the stock's highs, but its price is still in the top 25% of the daily bar's range.

2. An expansion-of-range-reversal retraces much of the constructive price action of the previous four days. The deepest bar in the pullback closes in the top of its range on solid volume. My plan is to enter .10 above the high of the bar labelled 2 in Figure 7.5.

3. CE triggers an entry and stops short of a full trip to the profit target, as the resistance experienced in the expansion-of-range-and-volume bar (1) is encountered again. A quarter point profit is booked for the trade.

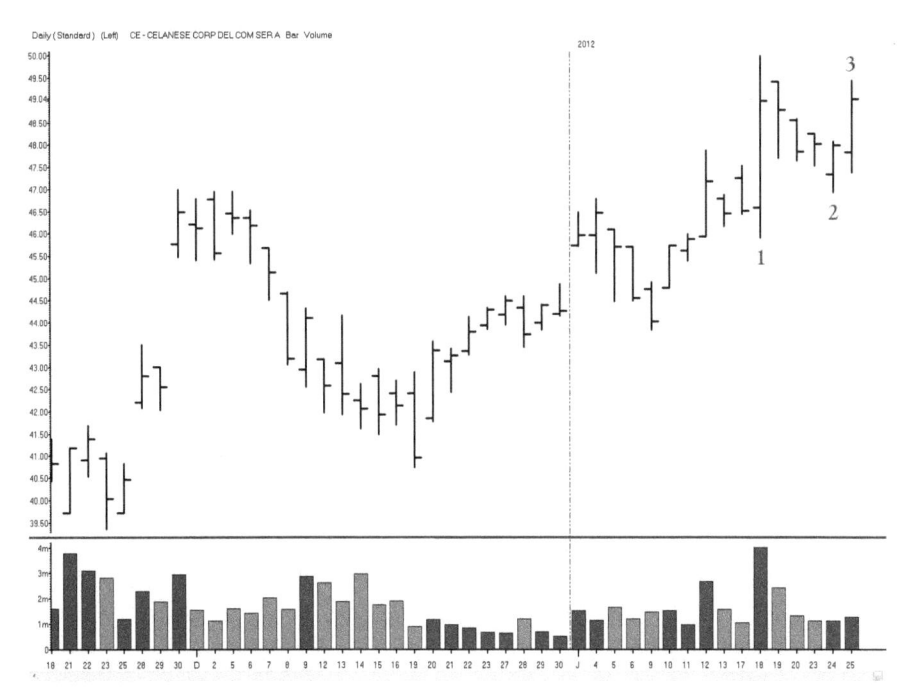

FIGURE 7.5 – CELANESE CORP.
RealTick by Townsend Analytics, Ltd.

Pullbacks do not have to be particularly deep to be significant. When a stock makes a large gap move that is followed by a shallow pullback, it indicates that a follow-through move may be in the making. Cimarex Energy Co. (XEC) provides a good example.

1. A large gap open pushes shares of XEC higher by $5 on the open.

2. The expansion-of-range-and-volume move adds $13 to the share price of XEC. The move also represents a gap-extension set-up.

3. A shallow pullback and continued strong buying interest. My expansion-of-range-reversal entry is planned for $81.24 the following day.

4. XEC triggers and closes $2 higher on the session.

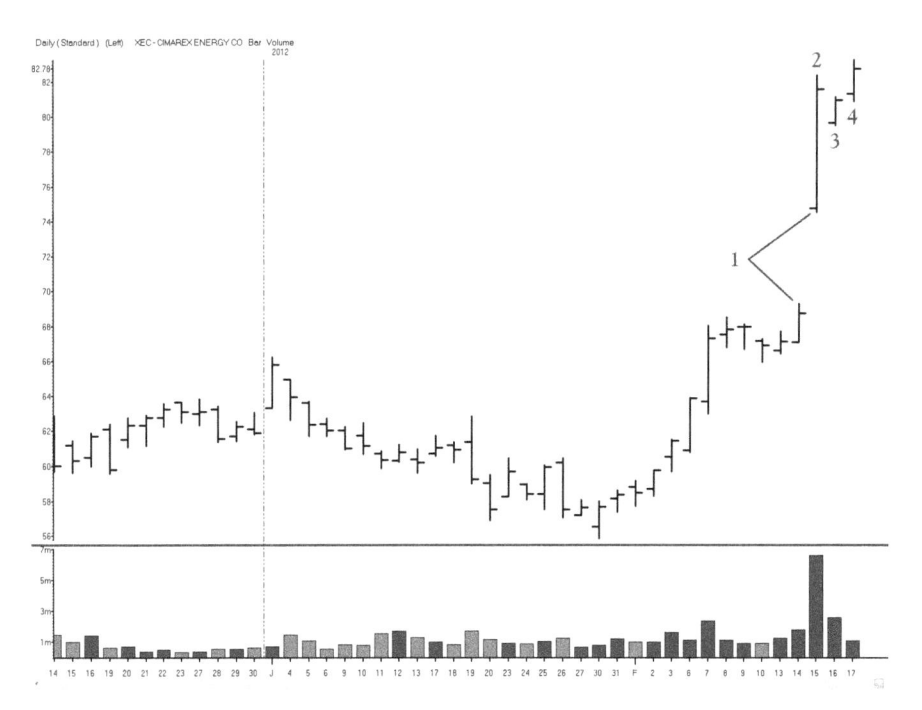

FIGURE 7.6 – CIMAREX ENERGY CO.
RealTick by Townsend Analytics, Ltd.

Although most traders equate surprises with nightmares, they do sometimes occur in your favour. Westlake Chemical Corp. (WLK) was a planned expansion-of-range-reversal trade on 2 August 2012. Before the open, the company reported results that beat consensus estimates by $0.31 per share. This made for a very good move over the course of the session.

1. An expansion-of-range-and-volume and gap-extension set-up forms on the WLK daily chart.

2. A three-day pullback sets up the expansion-of-range-reversal entry at $60.17. The stock closes low in the set-up bar, increasing the likelihood of an open below the trigger price.

3. WLK triggers and trades to $64.75.

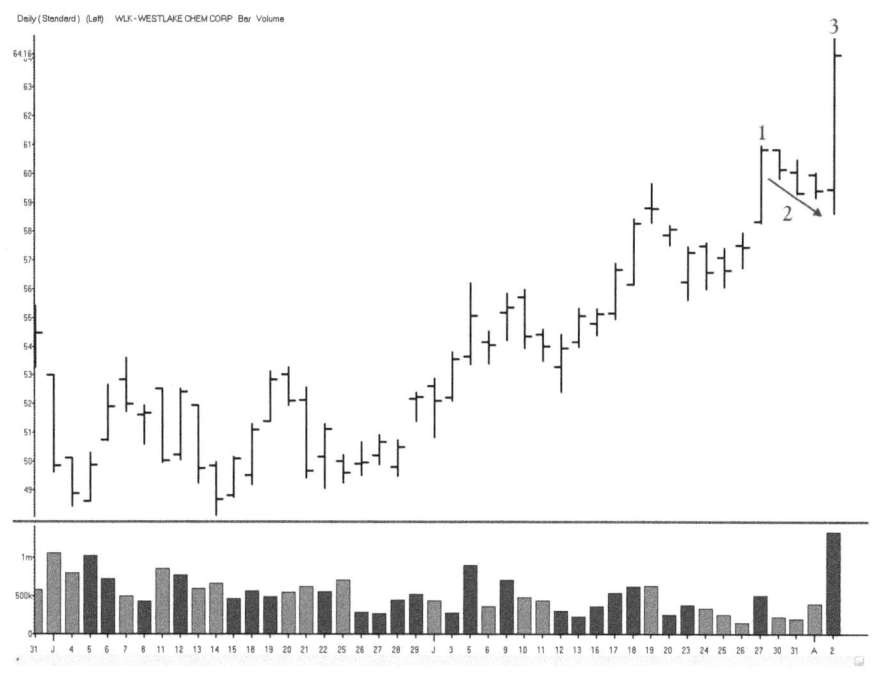

FIGURE 7.7 – WESTLAKE CHEMICAL CORP.
RealTick by Townsend Analytics, Ltd.

Summary

The expansion-of-range reversal is an important set-up for two reasons. First, it provides good intraday stability and profit potential when it triggers. I think this is because of the variety of market factors that are required for its formation. Second, it keeps us in a portion of the trade for what can often be a much larger move. This can contribute handsomely to long-term profitability.

The key to trading this pattern is patience. There are many false set-ups that continue to drift lower once they begin pulling back. This is particularly true in downward-trending markets. When everything falls into place, however, the expansion-of-range reversal makes for very good trading.

CHAPTER 8.
Expansion-of-Range-and-Volume Consolidations

P ATTERNS USUALLY DO not play out exactly the way we expect them to. Part of the job of a trader is to adapt to what is really happening instead of jumping every time there appears to be an opportunity. Every breakout trader eagerly anticipates the range expansion as a move with great potential. Many of us stop looking at these set-ups when they fail to immediately follow through, leaving what is possibly a great profit opportunity behind in the process. The expansion-of-range-and-volume consolidation pattern provides a second or third-day entry that can be more reliable than trading the anticipated follow-through day.

The basic premise here is that when range expansions occur, the market often needs time to digest the gains or losses. If the next trading day consists of a consolidation with an extreme close in the same direction as the expansion, a lucrative opportunity exists for a continuation move one or two days later.

The logic of the pattern is very easy to follow. We are basically looking for an expansion-of-range-and-volume set-up to fail to break out. We then want to see the momentum of the move cause directional energy to consolidate near the range extreme. Within a few days we look for entry as the pattern breaks in the direction of the momentum.

The example below illustrates the set-up for the long entry. The short entry works equally well, and is just the reverse. The rules are as follows:

1. On day one, an expansion-of-range-and-volume pattern sets up.

2. On day two (or as many as three additional days later) the stock should make a narrow range day, failing to substantially break the day-one high. The additional days in the pattern close in the top quarter of the expansion-of-range-and-volume day range.

3. On the trigger day, entry is .10 above the high of the expansion-of-range-and-volume day.

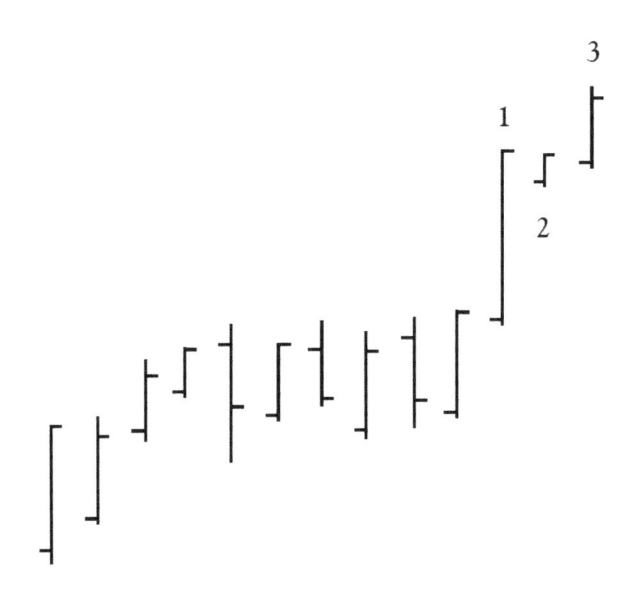

FIGURE 8.1

Aeropostale (ARO) traded lower from late April through May 2012. An expansion-of-range-and-volume move that was also a gap extension through the 200-period simple moving average (A) and the following days created an expansion-of-range-and-volume consolidation entry.

1. An expansion-of-range-and-volume move through the 200-period SMA.

2. The stock trades inside the high of the expansion-of-range-and-volume day's range.

3. An $18.13 entry triggers and the stock closes the session at $18.55.

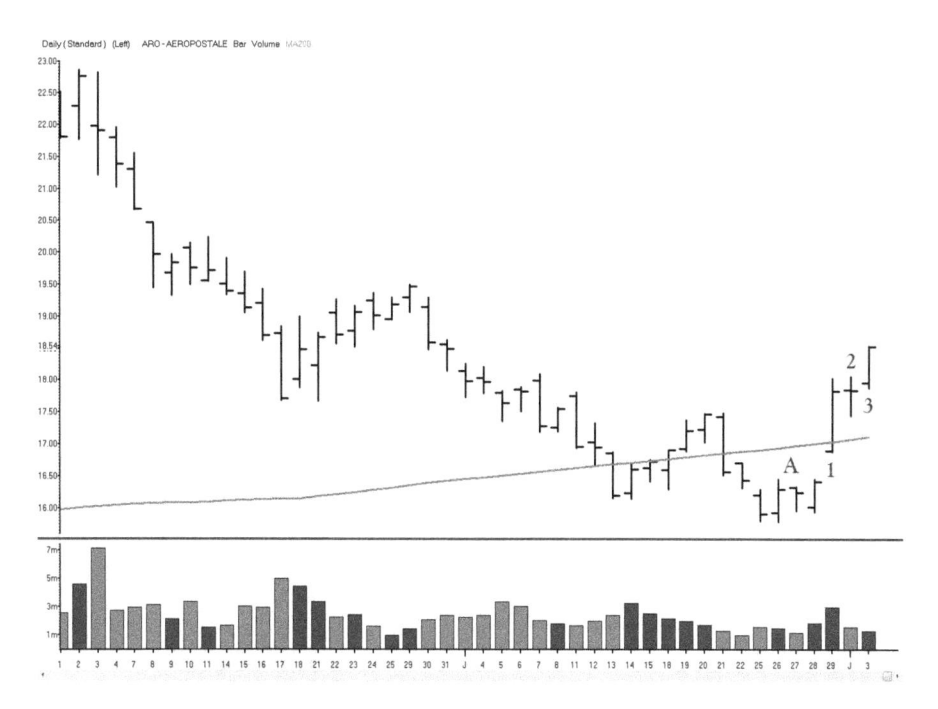

FIGURE 8.2 – AEROPOSTALE
RealTick by Townsend Analytics, Ltd.

A favorable FDA panel vote for Edwards Lifesciences' (EW) SAPIEN and FDA approval had analysts scrambling to raise price targets for the stock. This had an immediate impact on the stock's price, and had me eager to be part of any follow-through set-up.

1. An expansion-of-range-and-volume set-up after the positive news hits the newswires.

2. An inside day in the top of the previous session's range creates an expansion-of-range-and-volume consolidation planned entry at $99.10.

3. The stock trades through the trigger price and closes the session at $100.66.

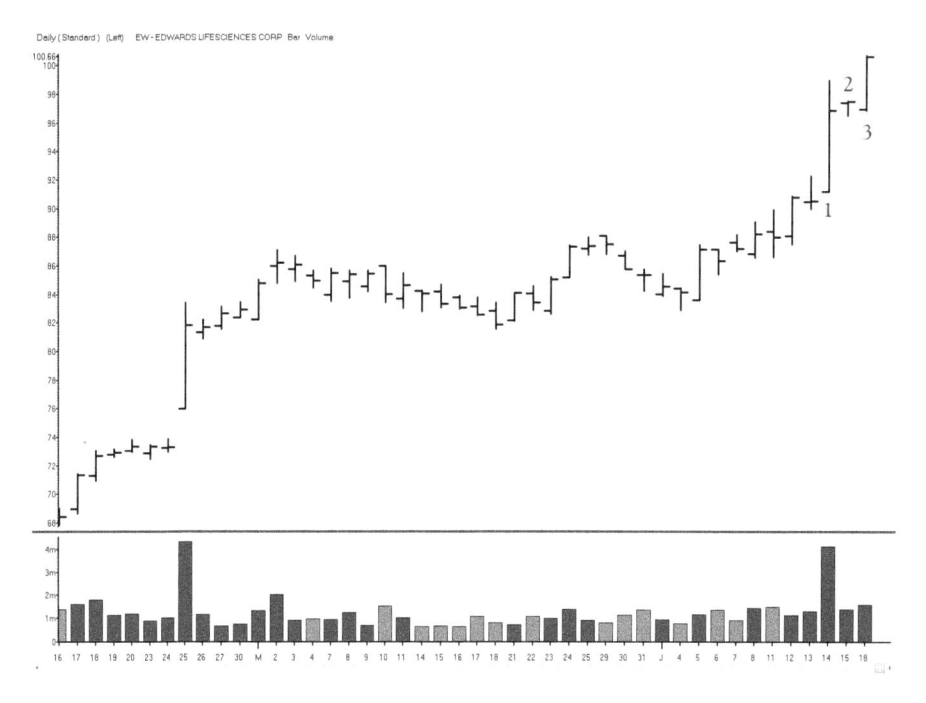

FIGURE 8.3 – EDWARDS LIFESCIENCES
RealTick by Townsend Analytics, Ltd.

Traders who subscribe to my trading plan frequently comment that some stocks seem to cycle almost endlessly, appearing on the plan many times over the course of a few months. Nuskin Enterprises (NUS) is one such stock. Over the course of two months in late 2011, NUS supplied several good trading opportunities.

1. An extension-reversal set-up forms after the previous session makes a wide-range move on heavy volume.

2. A profitable trade as the stock makes a $0.74 per share move to the short side.

3. An A–B–C ratio pullback is set for entry the following session.

4. The stock gaps beyond my allowable slippage and there is no trade on the session.

5. The C–D–E ratio pullback provides another trading opportunity. NUS moves $1.25 per share in favour of the trade.

6. A kings-and-queens reversal sets up, but NUS gaps lower in the following session and no trade is triggered.

7. An expansion-of-range-and-volume move lower. An entry is set for the following session on trade below $40.28.

8. NUS fails to trigger and forms an expansion-of-range-and-volume consolidation set-up. The entry is planned again for the following session at a violation of $40.28.

9. The short-sale trade triggers mid-morning and NUS moves lower to $39.12.

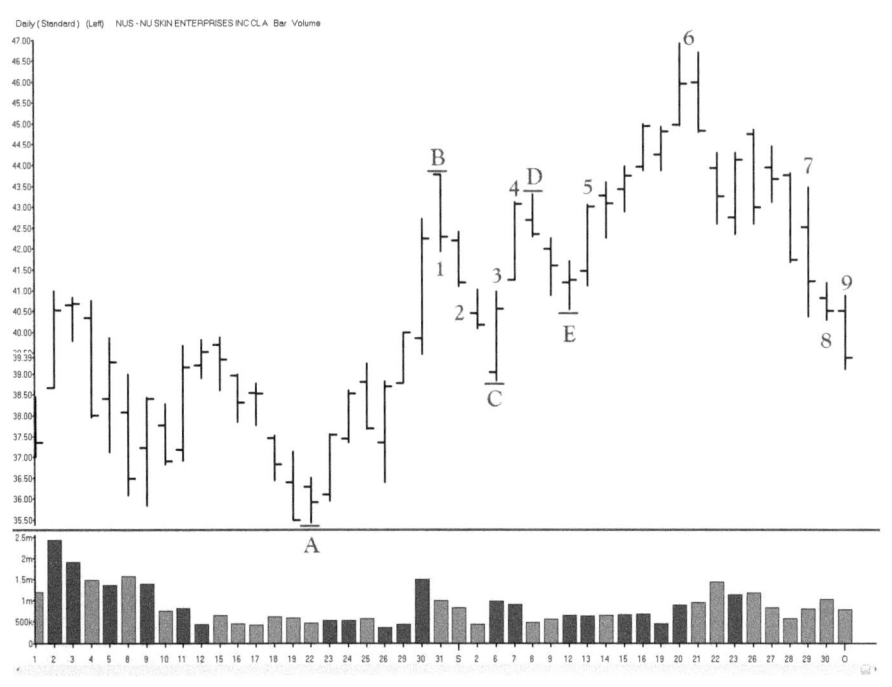

FIGURE 8.4 – NUSKIN ENTERPRISES
RealTick by Townsend Analytics, Ltd.

I generally do not like to trade expansion-of-range-and-volume set-ups after long sideways congestion ranges. There is a tendency for such ranges to draw price back in. I prefer to see the pattern develop into an expansion-of-range-and-volume consolidation prior to initiating a long or short trade, since this allows for conviction to become evident on the daily chart. While it would be ideal to see the set-up develop over a few days, Lennox International (LII) managed to set up as an intraday trade after just one inside day.

1. An expansion-of-range-and-volume closes off the stock's price highs, but it is still in the top 25% of the range.

2. An inside day in the top of the expansion-of-range-and-volume range develops. The potential expansion-of-range-and-volume consolidation entry is .10 above the expansion bar (1) in Figure 8.5.

3. A $41.41 entry triggers, and LII moves higher closing at $42.42.

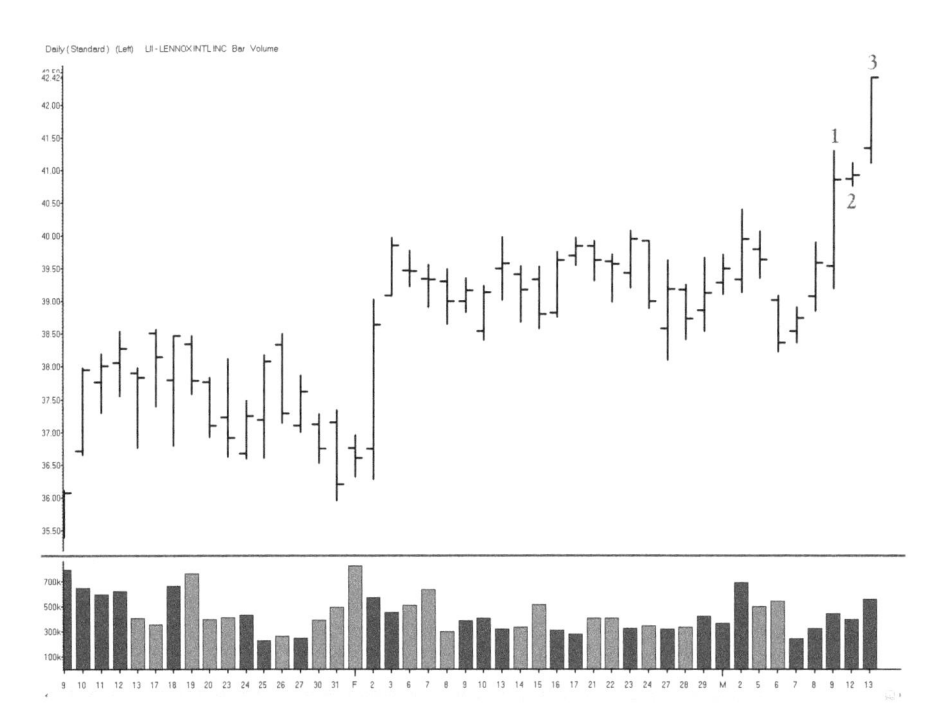

FIGURE 8.5 – LENNOX INTERNATIONAL
RealTick by Townsend Analytics, Ltd.

The short side of the market is always full of opportunity. Stocks tend to fall much faster than they climb; if the market is in a normal cyclical pattern, shorts almost always mean opportunity. When Jacobs Engineering Group Inc. (JEC) missed its consensus earnings figure on 30 April 2012, the stage was set for a move lower.

1. JEC gaps lower after announcing an earnings miss. The stock trades sideways for three sessions.

2. An expansion-of-range-and-volume bar breaks through the bottom of the range and closes at the top of the 2011 low range.

3. An inside day forms and the entry for the following session is planned for a violation of $38.97. This is below the low of the expansion-of-range-and-volume consolidation bar (3) not the expansion-of-range-and-volume bar. This level is chosen since the consolidation bar dipped slightly below the expansion bar.

4. The stock trades well below the initial profit target to $38.29 before reversing and closing only slightly lower on the session.

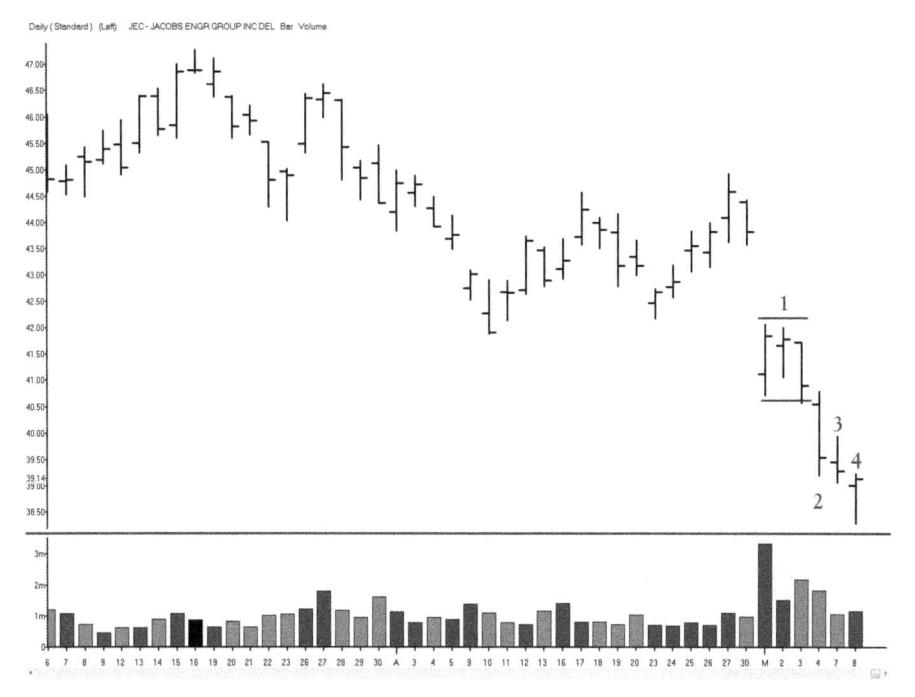

FIGURE 8.6 – JACOBS ENGINEERING GROUP INC.
RealTick by Townsend Analytics, Ltd.

8. Expansion-of-Range-and-Volume Consolidations | **69**

No news was good news for Ashland Inc. (ASH) in the summer of 2012, as the stock moved higher by nearly 10% in the span of just a few weeks. There were several opportunities to profit in ASH. The move in late August is a good example of an expansion-of-range-and-volume consolidation.

1. A sideways consolidation forms as traders seem to settle on a new value zone for ASH.

2. An expansion-of-range-and-volume bar breaks the stock up and out of the consolidation and over recent highs.

3. An inside day forms an expansion-of-range-and-volume consolidation set-up. The entry for the following session is $73.05.

4. The initial target for the trade is at pivot resistance 2. The stock climbs straight to this level at $73.49 before reversing to resistance 1. Much of the rest of the session is spent oscillating between the two resistance pivots.

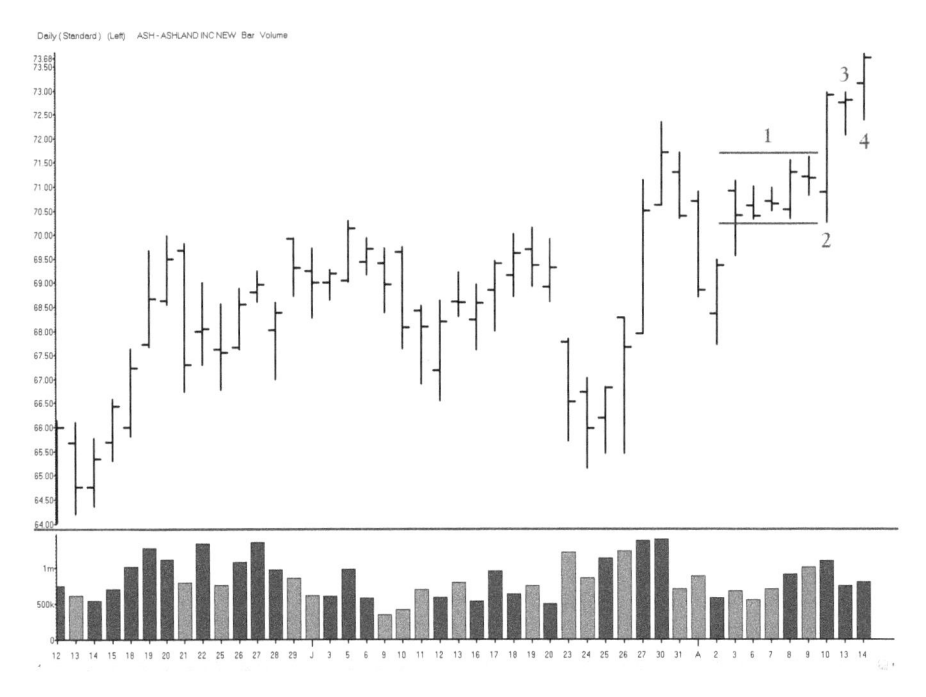

FIGURE 8.7 – ASHLAND INC.
RealTick by Townsend Analytics, Ltd.

Summary

Markets almost never do what we expect them to. Substantial price thrusts set the stage for additional profits, but often a few consolidation days are required for rapid advances or declines to lead to additional extensions. The expansion-of-range-and-volume consolidation gets us into the market at the right time by anticipating these two or three-day consolidations and waiting to trigger a trade until follow-through occurs.

CHAPTER 9.
Ratio Pullbacks

STRONG DIRECTIONAL MOVES are usually followed either by consolidation periods or pullbacks in the direction of the dominant trend. Although many traders advocate entering breakouts of these retracements the moment a higher tick is in place, better opportunities are to be had when some specific criteria are met. The ratio-pullback pattern focuses particular attention on the characteristics of the most extreme day of the move in an attempt to filter out pullbacks that lack the potential for follow-through. In doing so, many potential trend reversals are eliminated before they have a chance to cause losses. The ratio pullback is a pullback pattern that establishes a position after profit-taking has caused a one-to-five day correction in a trend. Several filters are used to differentiate the ratio pullback from moves with less profit potential.

First, the magnitude of the initial up or down wave should represent a minimum of 5% (10% for stocks priced under $40 per share) of the value of the equity being traded. This is important since the largest initial profit target we normally expect over several sessions in a pullback entry is a move back to the 100% extension of the initial wave. If we are trading a $30 stock that makes a move up to $33 and enter on a 50% pullback, our logical profit objective is 1.5 points. A 38.2% retracement would yield a target of approximately 1.15 points.

Now assume that our time frame has been shortened and we wish to take only an intraday position. While this reduces our risk, it also substantially tightens the profit objective. Logically planning the initial profit target for an intraday trade may only yield a move from the 50% retracement back to the 38.2% level established earlier in the correction. Thus, a 10% upward swing in a $30 stock yields a move of three points. A 50% retracement moves the stock down 1.5 points. Now, an intraday entry with an initial profit target around the earlier 38.2% level will yield approximately

.36 points on the trade. An initial move representing less than 10% of the value of the stock would not be worth the trouble or the risk of entering the position.

The second criterion I look for during the pullback is decreasing volume. Buying or selling pressure should always be greatest when price is moving in the direction of the 20-period SMA. If the volume during the corrective wave approaches that of the initial wave, then the trade has a lower probability of success than it does when volume increases as price moves in the direction of the underlying trend.

Third, I always examine the relative strength of the stock as reported in *Investor's Business Daily* prior to planning the trade. This trading strategy essentially seeks to buy strong stocks, or short weak ones, when they are compressed and ready to release some energy. Long-side candidates should have a minimum relative strength rating of 60. Conversely, short-sale set-ups should present relative strength readings of 30 or less.

The final step in picking the good set-ups is to examine the price behaviour of the most strongly correlated underlying sector. Thus if I am considering a trade in Anglogold Ltd (AU), I would look at the Philadelphia Stock Exchange's Gold & Silver Index (XAU.X) to determine whether or not AU is behaving erratically compared to its index.

All that being said, the ideal long set-up looks like the following chart. The rules for shorts are reversed.

1. A first move ends with a two-week high.

2. A correction takes price down as low as the 61.8% retracement and closes above its opening price, and preferably in the upper 25% of its range.

3. We open a position on trade above the high of the retracement low bar.

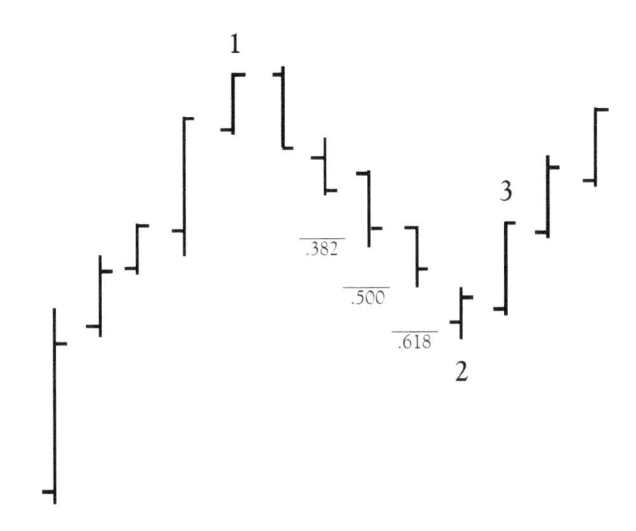

FIGURE 9.1

FTI Consulting (FCN) reported first quarter EPS of $0.43 versus consensus estimates of $0.61 in May 2012. The news sent the stock lower and prompted analysts to issue downgrades. Downgrades often lead to opportunities, and in this case a ratio pullback from recent lows had the stock on my trading plan for the day.

1. FCN moves lower from a swing high of $31.25 (A) to a swing low of $28.13 (B), then retraces 50% of the move and generates a ratio-pullback entry set-up at the deepest low in the pullback.

2. The entry at $28.88 travels smoothly to the support target at $28.25.

FIGURE 9.2 – FTI CONSULTING
RealTick by Townsend Analytics, Ltd.

Persistent directional moves against a backdrop of downgrades are not very common, but even as the analyst community suggested that it was overpriced, American Tower Corp (AMT) managed to trend higher in the summer of 2012. Options trading in AMT was at record highs, indicating that many traders thought there would be a surprise when the company reported earnings. These factors had me very interested in any pattern that set the stock up for an entry.

1. A 61.8% retracement of the A–B–C move sets up a ratio-pullback entry opportunity at trade .10 above the $67.77 high of the deepest bar in the pattern.

2. After a gap higher, AMT trades below the entry price then reverses and triggers an entry. The $68.47 resistance target is achieved in a heavily traded session.

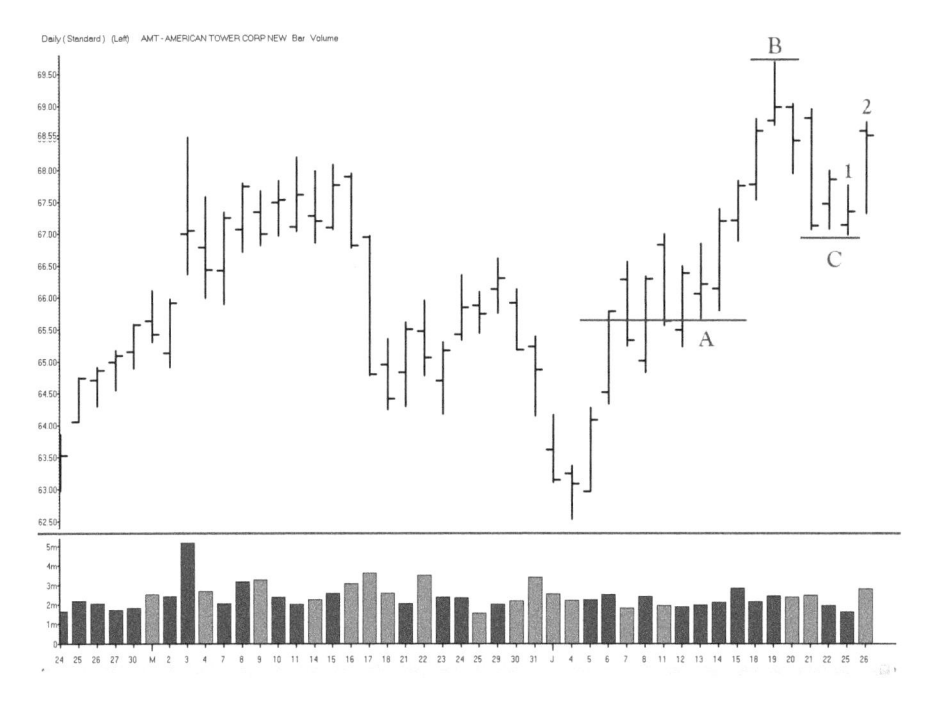

FIGURE 9.3 – AMERICAN TOWER CORP
RealTick by Townsend Analytics, Ltd.

An increasing pace of innovation had top-line sales growing rapidly at BorgWarner (BWA) in early 2012. Chatter about the company had many traders interested in the stock but opportunities for pattern entries were hindered by long periods of sideways consolidation and frequent gap reversals. When patterns did set up, however, BWA offered some very solid trades.

1. An A–B–C move does not result in a trade, as the stock gaps open beyond the entry and allowable slippage on the trigger day.

2. Staying with the stock as it makes another swing move (D–E–F) provides great results, as an entry above the 23 February 2012 high generates more than $2 per share in profits in just a few hours.

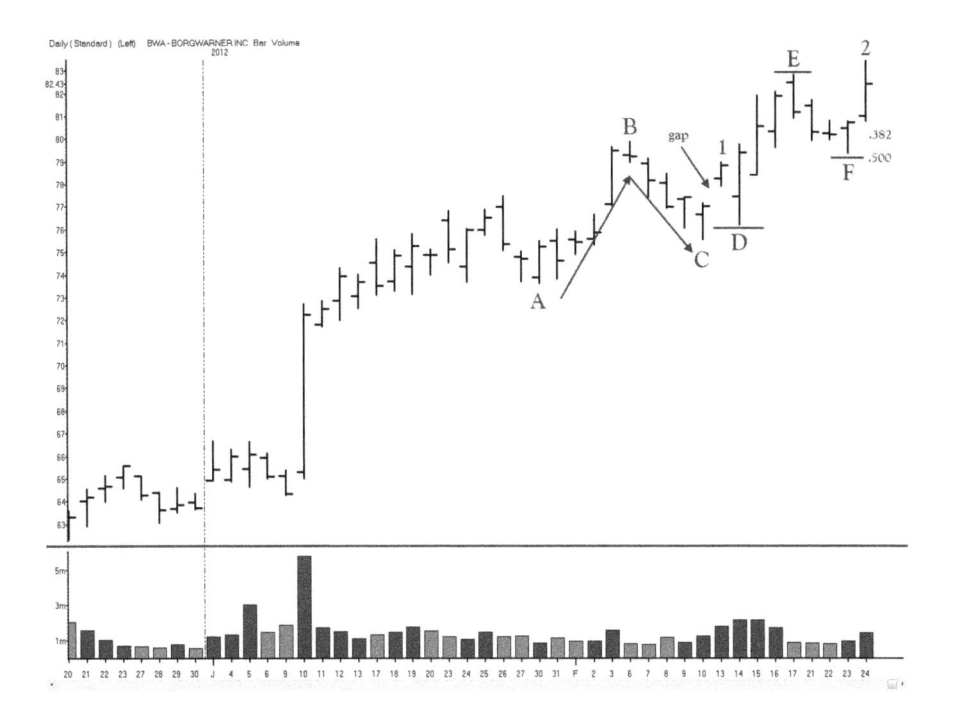

FIGURE 9.4 – BORGWARNER
RealTick by Townsend Analytics, Ltd.

Companhia Brasileira (CBD) is an ADR that I trade regularly. When the stock made a gap extension move followed by a ratio pullback, I was eager to capitalise on the power of the compound set-up.

1. A channel breakout forms both a gap-extension and an expansion-of-range-and-volume set-up.

2. The gap-extension trade follows through and delivers a profit-target extension.

3. The stock settles at a 38.2% retracement of an A–B–C swing move. An entry is planned .10 above the high of the daily bar.

4. The stock opens and triggers an entry almost immediately. The overhead resistance target is achieved, then CBD reverses and closes in the bottom of its range.

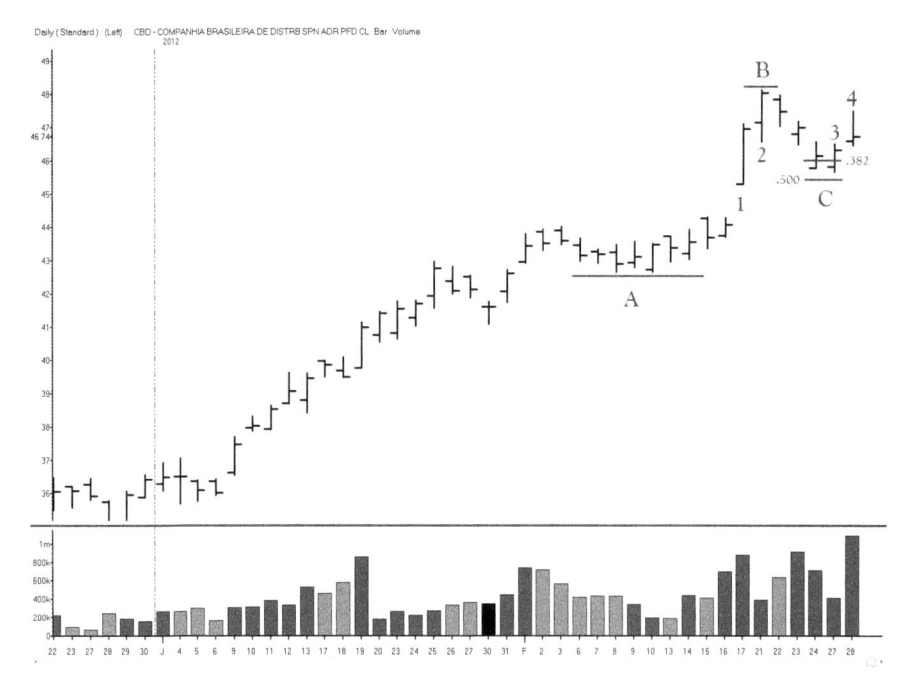

FIGURE 9.5 – COMPANHIA BRASILEIRA
RealTick by Townsend Analytics, Ltd.

Strong China comps and better general and administrative expenses had Wall Street bullish on shares of Yum Brands (YUM) in mid-2012. YUM offered many opportunities over the course of the year, with expansion-of-range-and-volume and ratio-pullback set-ups producing some of the best results.

1. YUM makes an expansion-of-range-and-volume move after positive analyst forecasts.

2. An expansion-of-range-and-volume consolidation set-up is followed by a profitable trade the next day.

3. A kings-and-queens-reversal set-up is followed by another profitable day of trading.

4. An A–B–C swing retraces 38.2% of the recent price appreciation creating a ratio pullback. An entry is planned for the following session.

5. The stock gaps higher then reverses below the entry price and triggers the planned position at $70.51. By the end of trading, the stock has exceeded the initial target and added $0.90 per share in profits.

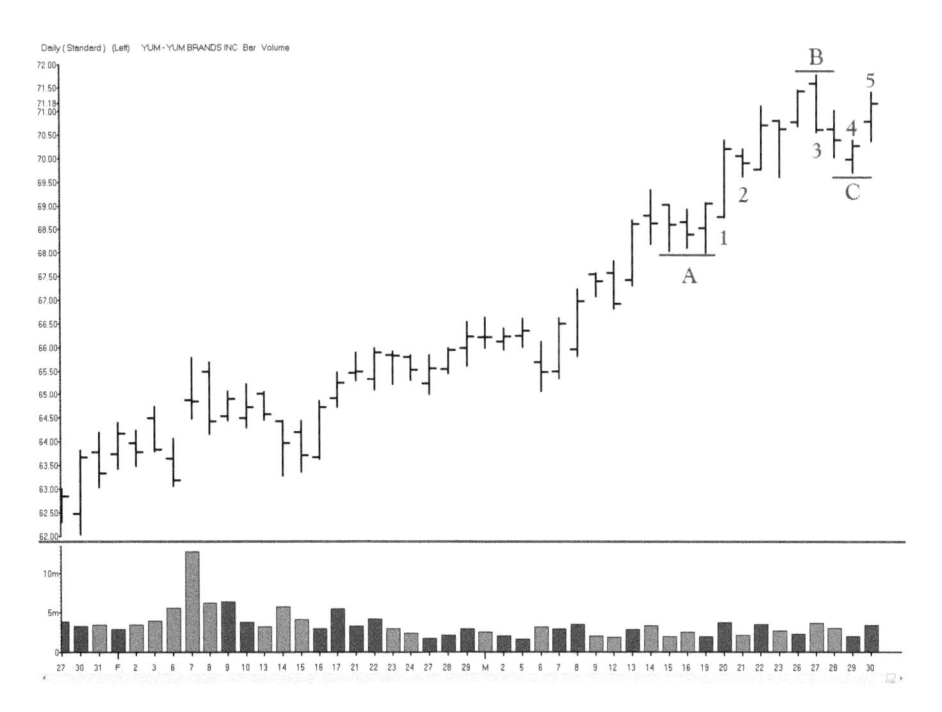

FIGURE 9.6 – YUM BRANDS
RealTick by Townsend Analytics, Ltd.

Cabot Oil & Gas (COG) announced many significant and potentially profitable joint ventures in 2012. When a pipeline announcement in late April sent the stock soaring there was solid trading on the horizon.

1. After an extension move higher, the stock completes an A–B–C swing and leaves a perfect 50% ratio pullback.

2. On the trigger day, the stock makes a $1.40-per-share move, nearly reaching the pinnacle of the swing high (B).

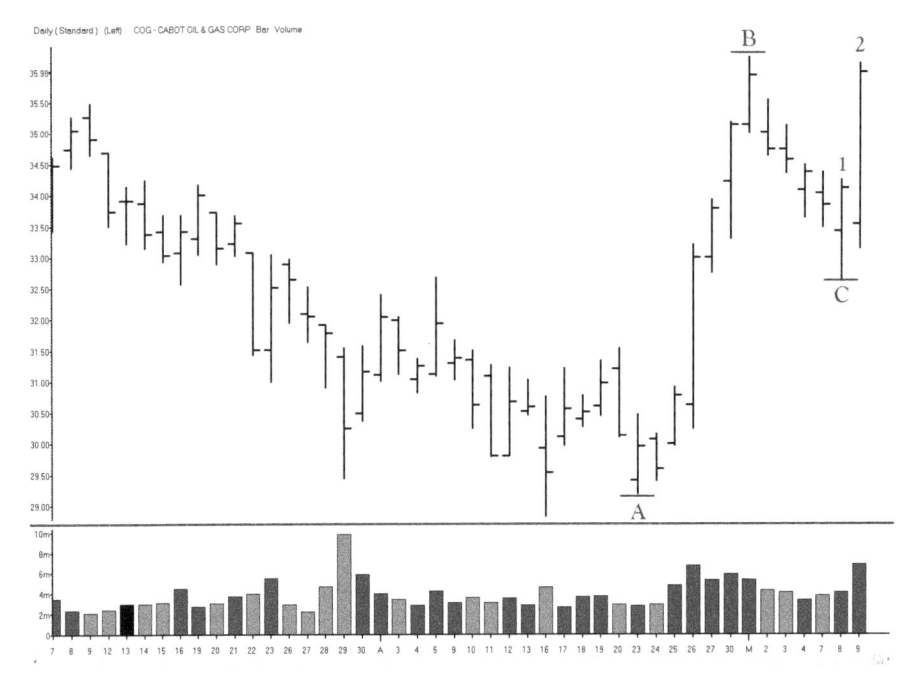

FIGURE 9.7 – CABOT OIL & GAS
RealTick by Townsend Analytics, Ltd.

Summary

If used with the proper discretion, pullbacks can yield solid gains. The key is recognising entries that represent pauses in the strongest moves. The ratio pullback takes a classic chart pattern and redefines it to make it stronger. Although the criteria limit the number of potential entries, the quality of the trades generated more than compensates for the reduction in their frequency. As intraday and swing techniques go, this one can yield impressive results. This is especially true when traders take the time to validate the underlying trend and make certain that sector correlations support any planned positions.

CHAPTER 10.
Kings and Queens

NOTHING LASTS FOREVER. The hottest stocks can suddenly drop precipitously on the most minor news. And even the worst stocks can turn around and climb higher when most of Wall Street has already prepared their eulogy. Kings and queens are daily reversal patterns that have the potential to generate good profits in the course of undoing recent price action. Although the greatest potential for this set-up is when it occurs as the last gasp in a pullback during an established trend, it also works well as a means of spotting and capitalising on the end of a move.

Charts are made up of large numbers of short waves that together form a longer-term trend. At the peak or valley of each of the short-term moves, we often find the kings-and-queens pattern signaling that a low or high has been put in. When this happens, a low-risk entry is presented, offering the alert trader the opportunity for intraday and multi-day profits. The pattern is easy to spot and generally pretty simple to trade.

The long and short trade set-ups are shown in the chart below.

1. Price moves to a low. Trading in the following session creates a near mirror image of the first day's move. Both bars should open and close near the extremes of their range. When both bars are in place the first criterion of the set-up is met.

2. The long entry is .10 to .15 above the high of the reversal bar. The profit target is A, the high of the bar on the day immediately preceding the set-up.

3. Price trends to an interim high. We wait until the reversal bar is in place, and the two bars together create the kings-and-queens confirmation.

4. The entry is .10 to .15 below the low of the reversal bar. The profit target is B, the low of the bar on the day immediately preceding the set-up.

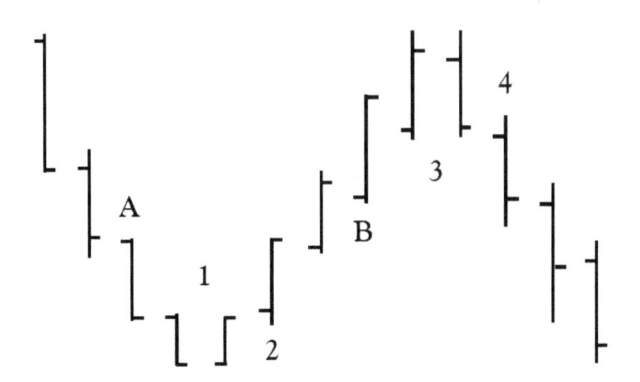

FIGURE 10.1

Terex Corporation (TEX) had a bullish year in 2012. The company announced lucrative joint ventures, was an analyst favorite, held opening gaps after upgrades, and maintained a persistent trend month after month. When a perfect kings-and-queens set-up presented itself in February it signalled either a short-term reversal or the beginning of a much larger move lower. In either case, the trade is a nearly picture-perfect example of what I am looking for with this set-up.

1. It is a beautiful start in 2012 for investors in TEX. The move higher starts in late December 2011 and doubles the stock's price by 21 February 2012.

2. A gap higher (A) closes solidly in the upper portion of the range. The next morning, however, profit-takers reverse the price action of the high bar and TEX leaves a kings-and-queens set-up on the day. An entry is planned for the following session if the stock trades to $25.55.

3. TEX hits its $25.10 initial profit target. It then reverses and closes flat on the session.

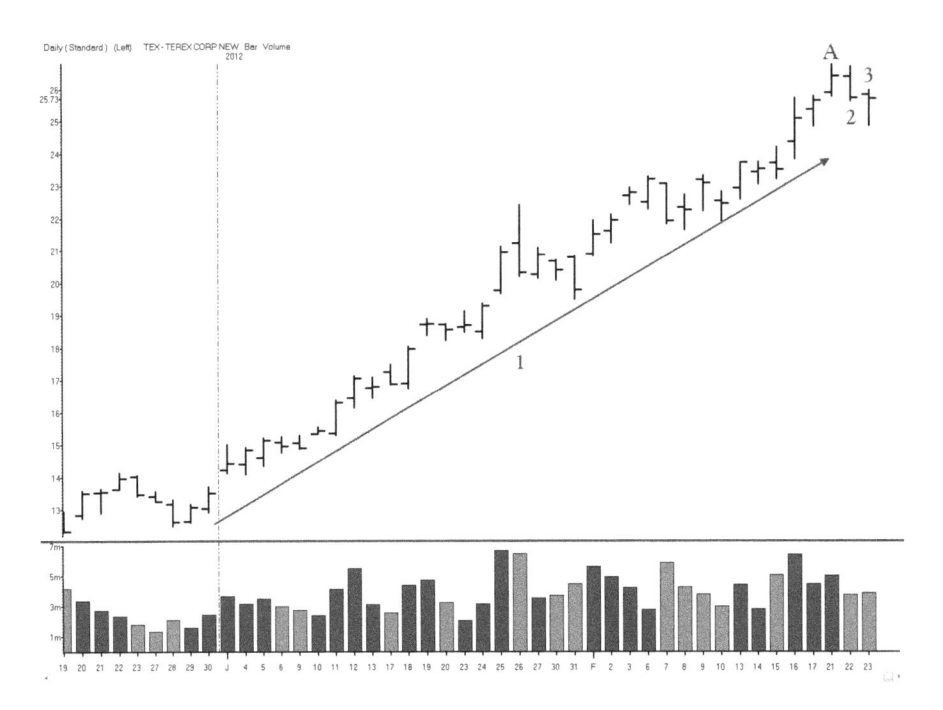

FIGURE 10.2 – TEREX CORPORATION
RealTick by Townsend Analytics, Ltd.

Compound set-ups are always promising. When they come on the heels of big trending moves, they tend to be indicative of a mean reversion in the making. Ethan Allen Interiors (ETH) provides a good example of such a scenario playing out.

1. A month-long slide shaves 20% off the value of ETH. The stock makes a swing low (B), then starts climbing higher. The reversal tops out with a 38.2% retracement of the A–B decline (C).

2. A kings-and-queens set-up forms. We plan a short sale-entry for the following session .10 below the low of the set-up bar.

3. After a $24.32 short-sale entry, the stock trades lower and closes at $23.61.

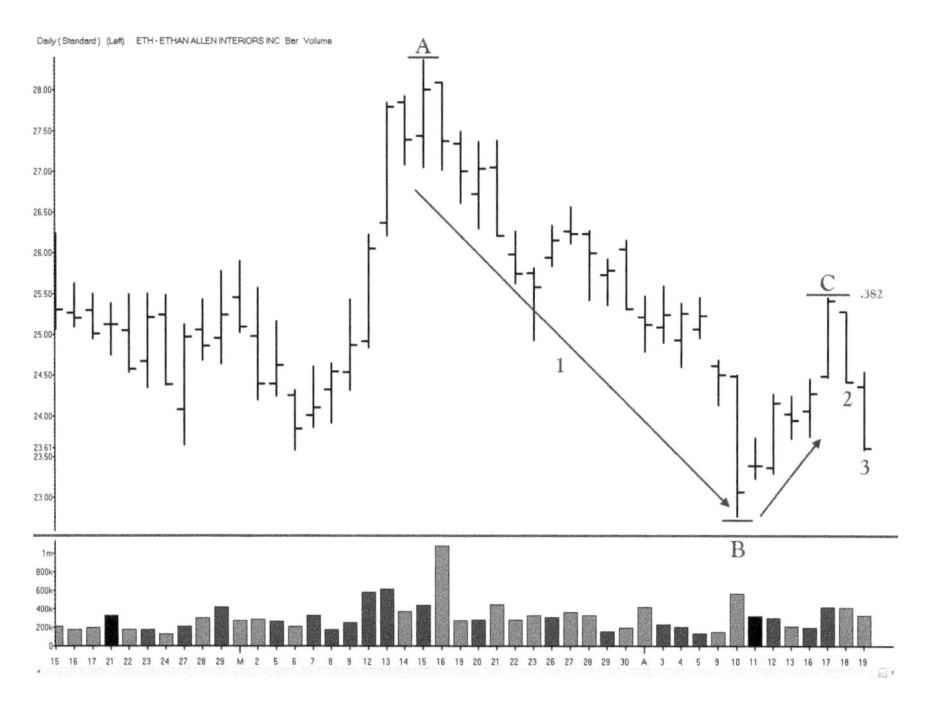

FIGURE 10.3 – ETHAN ALLEN INTERIORS
RealTick by Townsend Analytics, Ltd.

Minor moves can also lead to viable kings-and-queens set-ups. The pattern identifies profitable reversal patterns whenever a stock makes a move followed by a counter-move. The only time I will not consider a kings-and-queens trade is when the stock is trading in a sideways congestion range. FTI Consulting (FTI) provides a nice example of a low level set-up that leads to a profitable trade.

1. In an A–B–C move, FCN travels lower, then reverses and retraces 50% of the A–B leg. The move creates a kings-and-queens pattern with a short-sale entry .10 below the low of the 20 June 2012 bar.

2. The $28.88 short sale is followed by a move lower to $28.35, the precise level identified as a support target.

FIGURE 10.4 – FTI CONSULTING
RealTick by Townsend Analytics, Ltd.

High-volume selling after a significant move higher generally indicates that pressure will continue throughout several trading sessions. Crown Castle International Corp. (CCI) had a fast run higher in mid-June 2012, and then a heavy-volume sell-off. The trade is demonstrative of what a daily chart should look like when planning a kings-and-queens day trade.

1. CCI makes a sharp move higher and a low-volume thrust (A) that closes in the top of its range.

2. A kings-and-queens reversal on heavy volume triggers an entry at $57.40.

3. The short sale triggers and the stock trades lower to $56.92, a $0.01 extension of the initial support target.

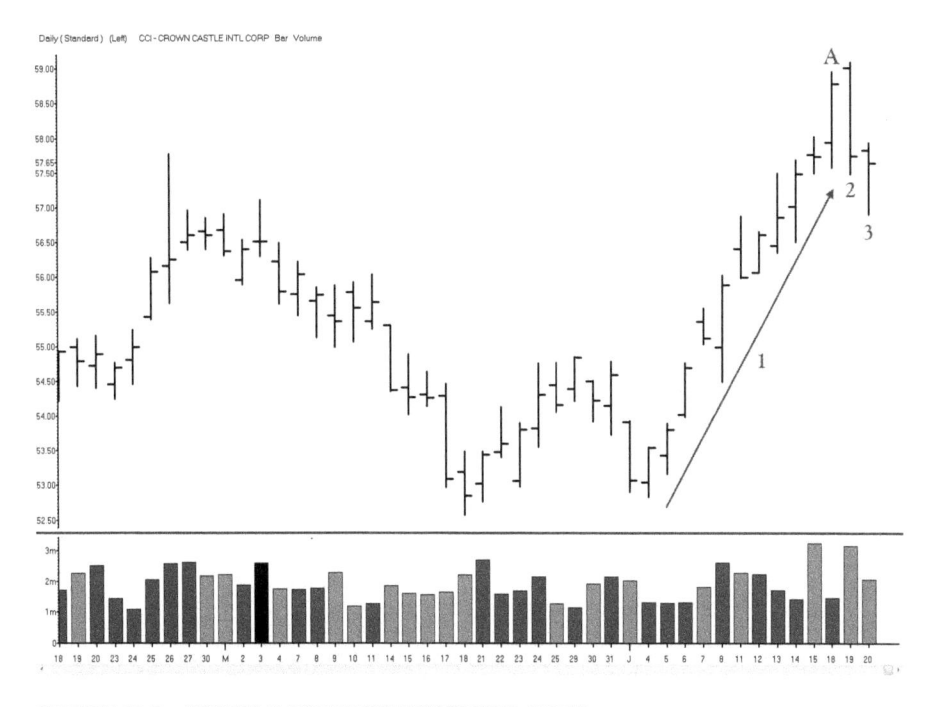

FIGURE 10.5 – CROWN CASTLE INTERNATIONAL CORP.
RealTick by Townsend Analytics, Ltd.

Hospitality Properties Trust (HPT) is a good example of traders buying the rumour and selling the news. Although the stock managed to beat the street consensus in early May 2012, a 20% mark-down was the ultimate outcome. A kings-and-queens pattern presented itself in early June, with a clear overhead resistance target and very clean pattern dynamics in the set-up.

1. HPT slides $5 and makes a low on decreasing volume.

2. The kings-and-queens set-up bar forms on heavy daily volume, indicating good potential for follow-through.

3. A $22.87 entry is triggered early in the session. The stock never looks back. By the end of the day HPT is trading at $23.36.

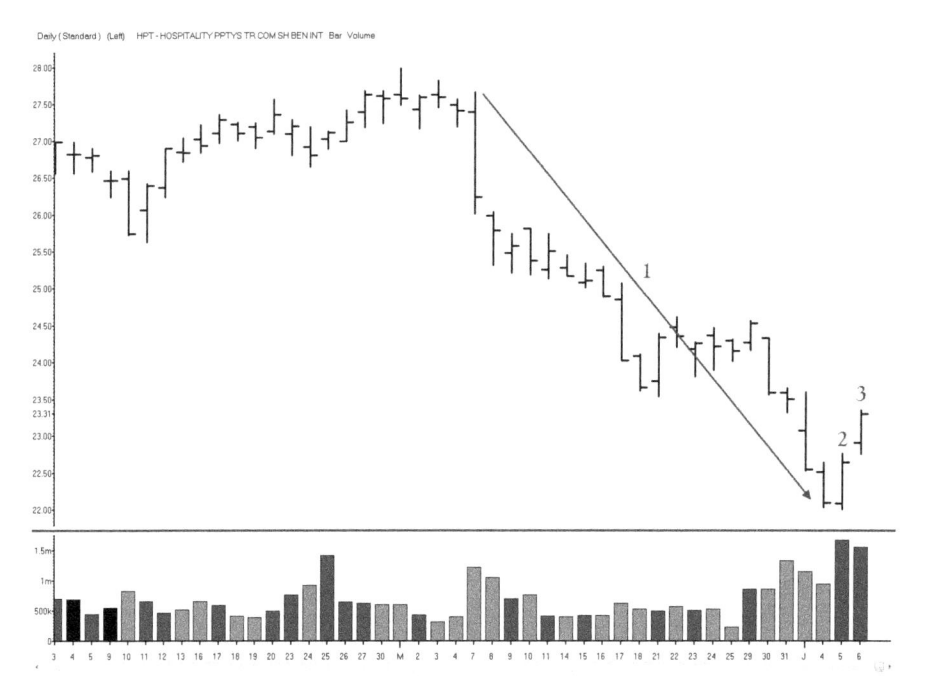

FIGURE 10.6 – HOSPITALITY PROPERTIES TRUST
RealTick by Townsend Analytics, Ltd.

Stocks definitely have personality characteristics, just like the people who trade them. Some are prone to repeating the same price behaviour over and over again; Agilent (A) is one such stock. Repeated set-ups for intraday trading are very common across the universe of stocks that I trade. In Figure 10.7, multiple kings-and-queens set-ups present themselves and trigger over the course of a month.

1. Agilent makes a kings-and-queens low (A) after sideways trading in a four-point range. A move above the trigger price results in an $0.70-per-share gain (B).

2. Just over a week later, another kings-and-queens low (C) results in another $0.70 per share gain (D).

3. A kings-and-queens top (E) is followed by more than one dollar in short-sale profits.

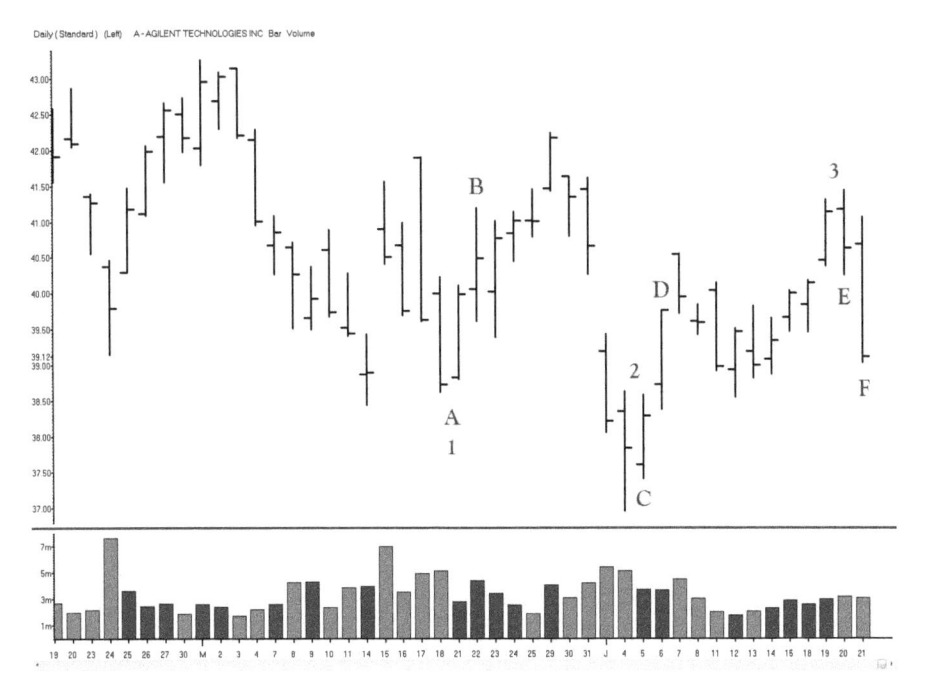

FIGURE 10.7 – AGILENT
RealTick by Townsend Analytics, Ltd.

Summary

The kings-and-queens pattern provides an excellent means of identifying reversal moves as they are forming, rather than attempting to jump on board in the days that follow. When it triggers, it is generally easy to catch, and when it fails, kings and queens tends not to get us in at all. The pattern does not present itself as frequently as some of the others presented in this text, but when it does I find it reliable and, best of all, profitable. The parameters of the set-up are a little trickier to program for computer scanning than some, but chart-flipping for these is relatively easy because of their distinctive appearance.

CHAPTER 11.
Deferred Set-ups

THE BEST TRADING plans often turn into piles of scrap paper when nothing hits on trigger day. Sometimes, though, opportunity knocks twice and a great trade emerges late from a plan that seemingly failed us. I call these situations deferred set-ups. They demonstrate how vigilance can generate profits.

I am including my deferred set-ups strategy to focus on the fact that the business of equities trading requires flexibility. Deferred set-ups are actually an extension of each of the daily patterns, but since they require intraday monitoring and strategising they are included in this section. Days on which few or no trades trigger could easily be forgotten. What I do instead is take the set-ups that did not blow out against the plan and save them for the next day or two.

Much of what we do requires the cooperation of the market. My plans are almost always for continuation entries in the direction indicated by a stock's fundamentals, relative strength and multiple-time-frame trend. If we plan for an entry on a break outside a tight consolidation range and there is no trigger, that plan does not become invalid. The stock simply took a breather. The only reason I would eliminate a non-trigger from the radar is if a move completely contrary to the trend and the planned entry occurred. If it looks like a reversal, it's usually a good idea to back off.

Most of the set-ups in this book lend themselves to deferred set-up entries. An expansion-of-range-and-volume consolidation is, of course, a variety of the expansion-of-range-and-volume, and is itself a deferred set-up. The expansion-of-range-and-volume consolidation, extension reversal, the gap extension, the expansion-of-range reversal, and the ratio pullback all provide very good second-day entry opportunities. Again, the distinction between deferred set-ups and a pattern failure is that the latter occurs when there has been a violation of the set-up day criteria. We *never* look to enter a pattern-failure continuation. We only take the deferred set-up entry when the stock has done nothing wrong. It simply took a day or two to pause.

In this chapter, I will show you some actual deferred set-up triggers that occurred in 2012 based on patterns that were identified for the previous day in my intraday trading service. As you examine each one, remember we are looking for the spirit of the set-up to remain unaffected by the previous day's failure to trigger.

Keeping an eye open for deferred set-ups is a good way to add profits to your bottom line. I strongly suggest that you add this simple strategy to your trading arsenal.

An Oppenheimer downgrade of New Oriental Education (EDU) is the latest in a series of negative news releases regarding the company, and a move lower was followed by a retracement move that seemed to fail to follow through.

1. A swing move in A–B–C generates a ratio pullback set-up.

2. The stock fails to trigger an entry on the planned trigger day.

3. One day later, EDU trades lower through the short-sale trigger and travels more than $0.40 per share in our favour.

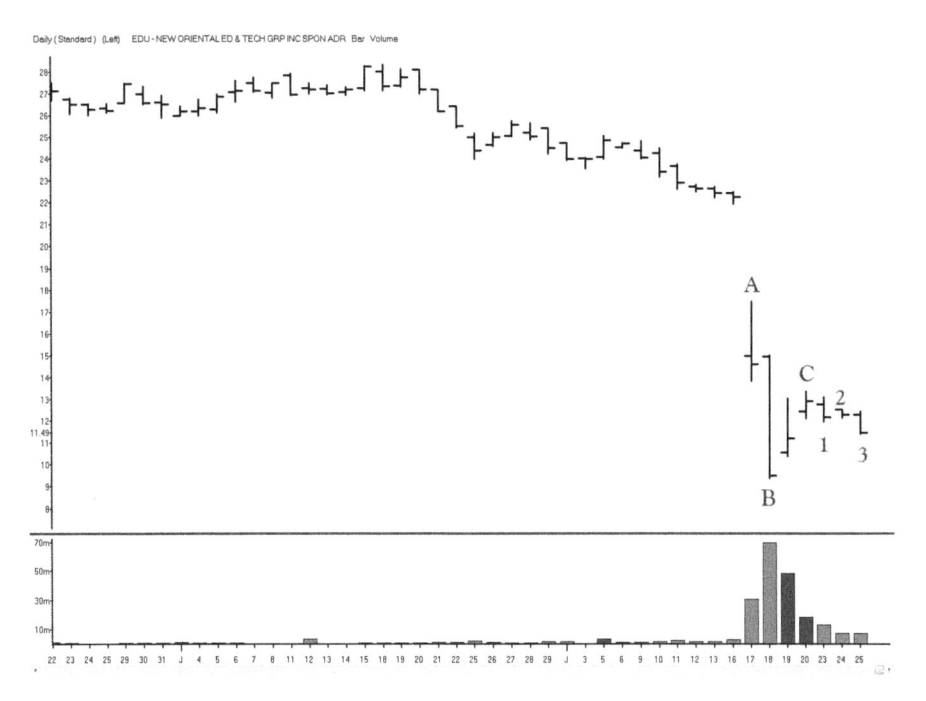

FIGURE 11.1 – NEW ORIENTAL EDUCATION

11. Deferred Set-ups | **93**

Sometimes a failed ratio pullback set-up gives way to a deeper ratio pullback. Staying vigilant after a trade fails to trigger and not being discouraged is the only way to get in front of the opportunity. This is illustrated in the example of Devry Inc. (DV).

1. A swing move in A–B–C results in a ratio pullback that fails to trigger an entry.

2. The ratio pullback extends from 50% to 61.8%, and we plan another entry.

3. DV delivers a $0.90 per share short-side move.

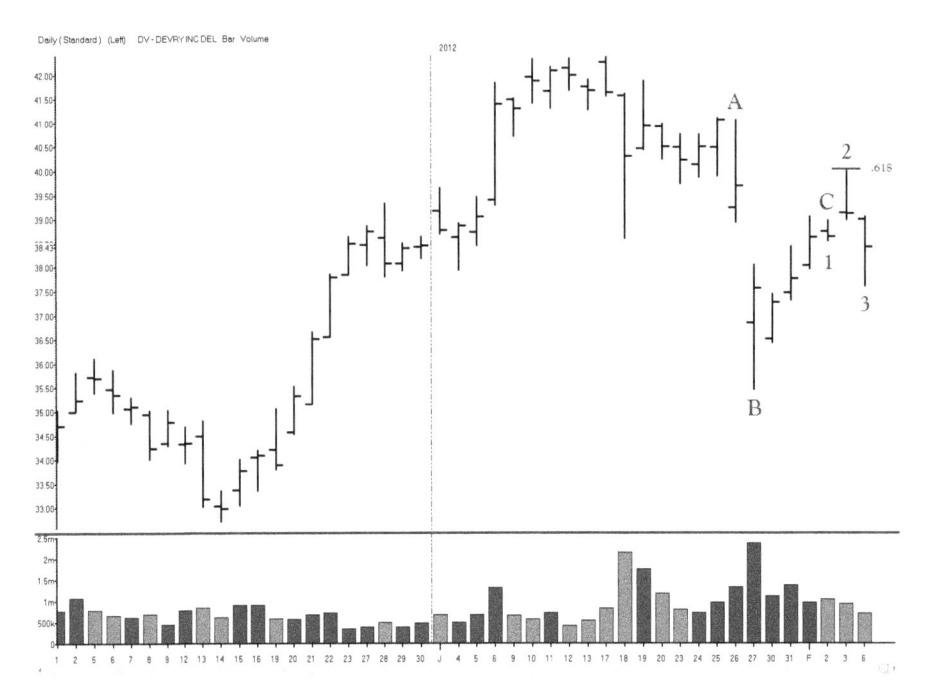

FIGURE 11.2 – DEVRY INC.
RealTick by Townsend Analytics, Ltd.

Most of the trades presented in this book represent ideal set-ups. I do, however, also plan entries when everything is less than perfect. Monster Beverage Corp (MNST), a NASDAQ stock that I frequently trade, provides a solid example of this.

1. A kings-and-queens set-up has a single bar between the mirror-image days. The bar opens and closes at the same price, and when the reversal bar follows a day later (A), I elect to plan the long-side trade based on the spirit of the move.

2. On the planned entry day, the stock fails to follow through. It does not significantly violate the high of the bar that completed the pattern (A). I plan for another potential entry a day later.

3. The stock triggers an entry on 16 August 2012 and travels $1.61 per share in my favour.

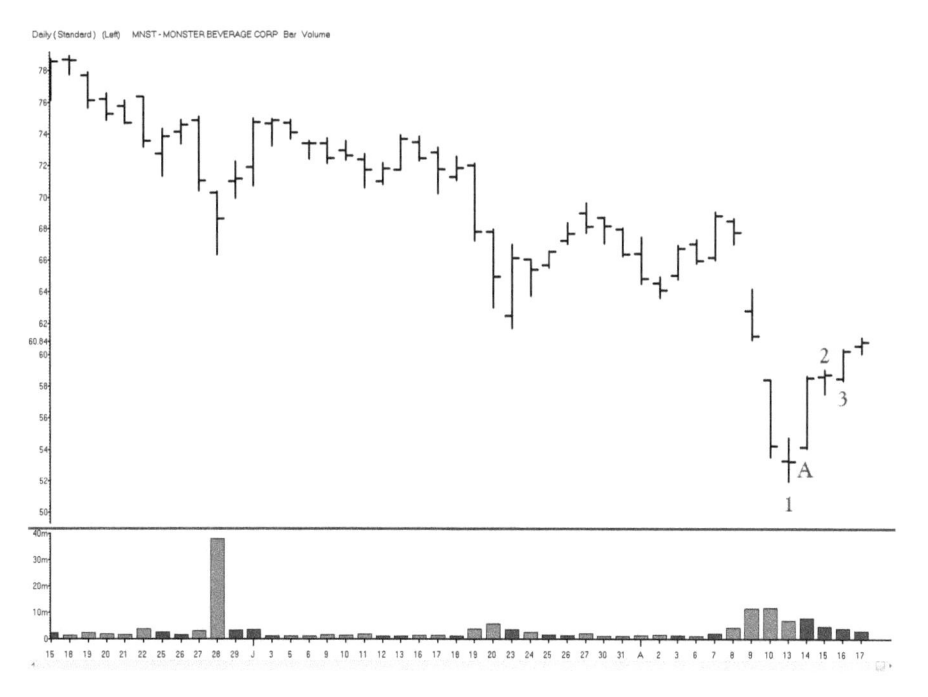

FIGURE 11.3 – MONSTER BEVERAGE CORP
RealTick by Townsend Analytics, Ltd.

Brookdale Senior Living Inc. (BKD) provides an example of an expansion-of-range-and-volume set-up that became an expansion-of-range-and-volume consolidation, and then continued on in the spirit of the set-up, even though a higher-range consolidation formed. This type of secondary set-up is less common than some of the others in this chapter, but it demonstrates again the importance of flexible thinking when evaluating potential trades.

1. An expansion-of-range-and-volume bar also qualifies as a gap extension.

2. The set-up fails to trigger. An expansion-of-range-and-volume consolidation forms.

3. BKD trades above the expansion-of-range-and-volume consolidation high for a small profit. The stock then begins a new consolidation range (A) that is supported by the highs of the previous range (2).

4. An entry on a breakout of the range highs travels $1.09 in our favor before retracing slightly into the close.

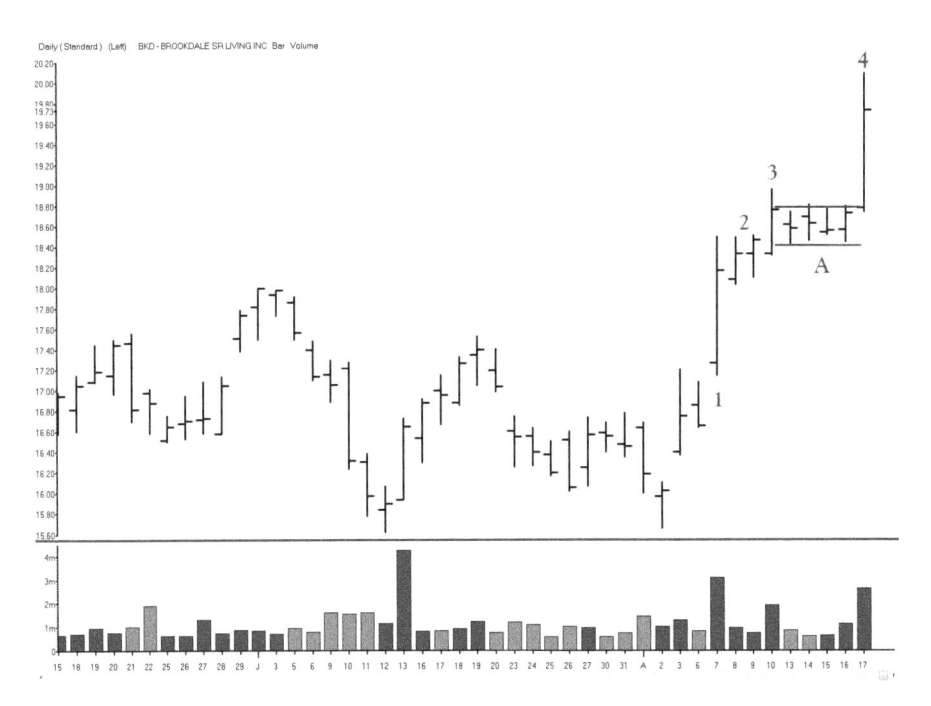

FIGURE 11.4 – BROOKDALE SENIOR LIVING INC.
RealTick by Townsend Analytics, Ltd.

Better-than-expected earnings sent shares of Carter Inc. (CRI) soaring higher in a gap expansion move that led to profits only after two failed triggers.

1. CRI announces earnings that beat consensus estimates. The stock gains over $4 in a single trading session, and leaves a gap-expansion set-up.

2. CRI opens slightly higher, moves to the trigger price, but fails to follow through.

3. A ratio pullback and an entry is planned .10 above the high of the daily bar with a target in the closing range of the gap-expansion bar (1).

4. The stock failed to reach the target on the trigger day (A), but did not engage in any deconstructive price activity. After setting a new entry at .10 above the previous day's bar (A), CRI travels beyond the profit target, locking in gains with a reversal of two closes.

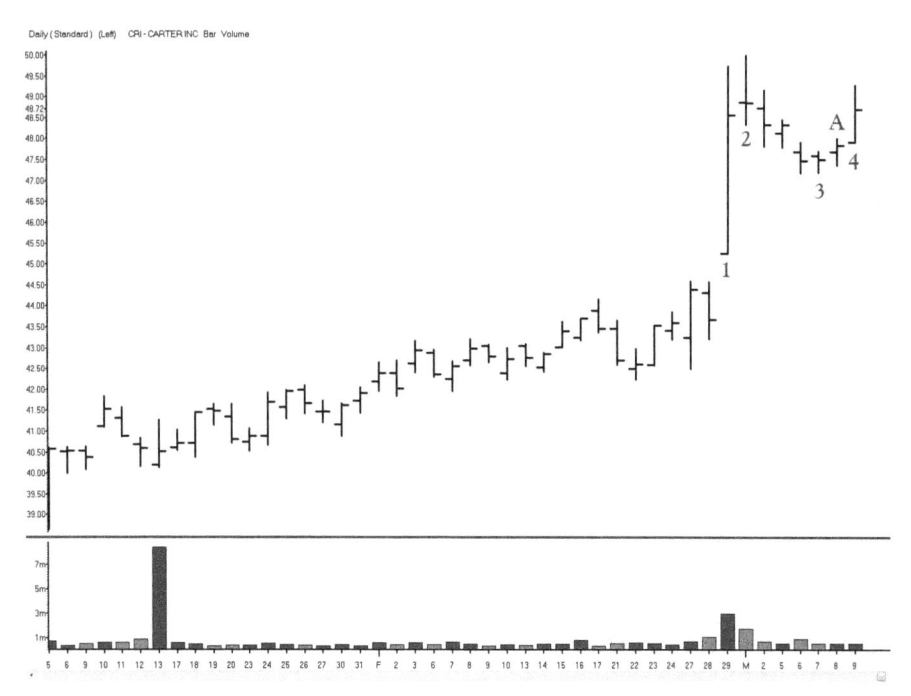

FIGURE 11.5 – CARTER INC.
RealTick by Townsend Analytics, Ltd.

News about a potential end to the uncertainty surrounding Greece in the Eurozone sent shares of Royal Bank of Canada (RY) creeping higher in early March 2012. Several opportunities for trades presented themselves over the course of the month, with some good examples of deferred set-ups.

1. A gap expansion move happens on the trigger day of a ratio pullback. The stock closes in the top of the range, and an entry is planned for the following day.

2. RY triggers an entry, but closes near flat for the session.

3. After another flat close (A), an entry is planned again .10 over the high of the gap expansion (1). The stock trades to the top of the 29 February 2012 high and breaks out, gaining over $1 per share on the trade.

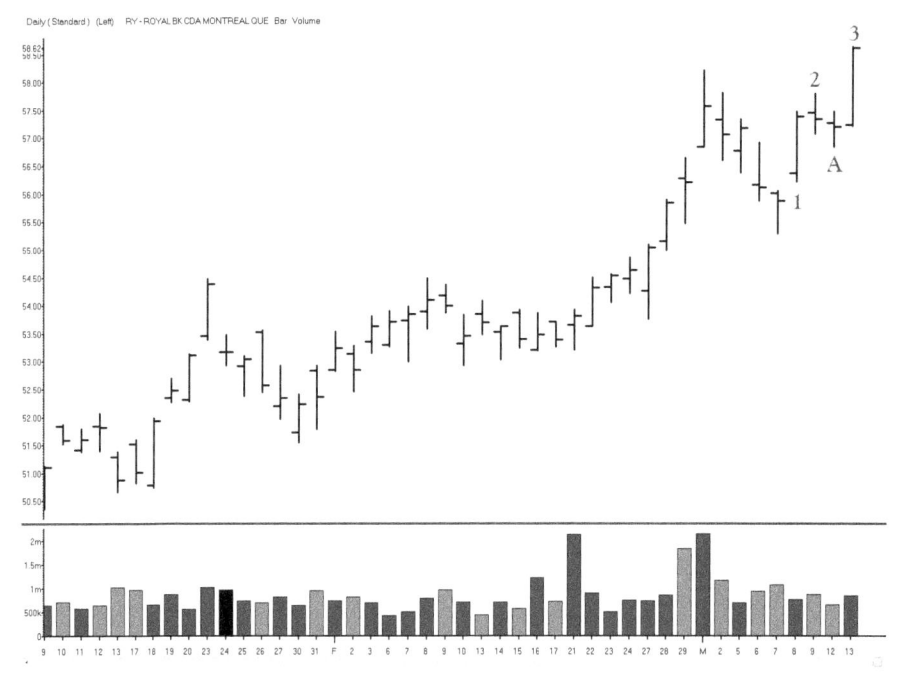

FIGURE 11.6 – ROYAL BANK OF CANADA
RealTick by Townsend Analytics, Ltd.

Four downgrades in the month of June sent shares of Basic Energy (BAS) lower early in the summer of 2012. The descent was on heavy volume, and tracked tightly with the mean price as the stock moved lower.

1. A move to the downside has BAS hugging its progressively lower mean from the time the stock is downgraded until there is some relief in the form of a first upgrade being issued (B). This has investors looking for an entry and signs that a low has been put in.

2. The stock traded higher and formed a ratio pullback (C) which triggered but stopped out for a loss. In the two days that followed, the ratio pullback deepened, providing another entry set-up below the low of the deepest bar (D).

3. BAS gaps lower and triggers an entry after retracing some of the morning's decline. The day's price action leads to a profit-target exit. BAS closes trading off the lows of the day.

FIGURE 11.7 – BASIC ENERGY
RealTick by Townsend Analytics, Ltd.

Summary

Deferred set-ups emphasise that, as traders, we must have the courage and conviction to follow our plan through to its logical conclusion. Sometimes our plans do not execute as expected. That does not mean that it is time to scrap all of the careful planning. Rather, we need to be willing to look for opportunity when it is located in the most obscure of all places – right in front of us.

CHAPTER 12.
Opening-Gap Reversals

TRADING THE OPEN can make for a very rough ride. Things can get particularly hairy when there is a significant gap due to erratic behaviour in the overnight futures markets. The opening-gap reversal is an intraday pattern that uses basic statistics and five-minute bars to find a high-probability turning point after an overreaction opening. It is easiest to execute as a long strategy from a sharp gap-down open, but it works equally well as a short sale. The only caveat is that if there are a lot of traders shorting the move, you sometimes have trouble getting quick fills.

The opening-gap reversal relies on some basic principles of statistics to derive a set-up. For those of you who shudder at the very thought of mathematics, take a deep breath and rest assured that it's going to be all right: the concepts that need to be understood are the most fundamental computations in any first-year university text on the subject. That being said, there are three inputs that are required to compute the parameters for trade entry. The first is the standard deviation (SD). The formula is as follows:

$$SD = \sqrt{\text{average of (deviations from average)}^2}$$

In this case, the average we are using in the calculation of SD is the mean value of true range, which represents price volatility by calculating the difference between the true range high and the true range low. To perform the calculation for each day in a series, note the current bar's high or the previous close, whichever is greater. Call that value TRH. Next, note the current low or the previous close, whichever is lower. Call this value TRL. Now perform the simple calculation TRH - TRL and voilà, true range!

Now comes the fun part. We will walk through the process of performing the calculations for validating the pattern. Once this portion of the chapter is completed, you should be able to enter the formulas into your real-time charting software and obtain alerts when any of the stocks on your scan-list meet the criterion established.

Let's use some actual recent data to perform the calculation. The time period is 10–23 August 2012. The market was trending strongly, with minor S&P resistance near the 1418 level. Gap openings occurred regularly, and movement in the S&P 500 futures acted like a magnet to pull the gap-down openings up and the gap-up openings down. This made for a good trading environment, with the dominant trend being a good predictor of follow-through, and countertrend opportunities also present if we were looking for them.

The stock we will examine in the example is Urban Outfitters (URBN). The true range values have already been calculated and are as follows:

	Urban Outfitters Inc. NASDAQ : URBN		
	8/7/2012	0.94	
	8/8/2012	0.44	
	8/9/2012	0.36	
	8/10/2012	0.47	
	8/13/2012	0.66	
	8/14/2012	0.63	
	8/15/2012	0.98	
	8/16/2012	0.46	
	8/17/2012	0.82	
	8/20/2012	0.89	

TABLE 12.1 – URBN TRUE RANGE DATA

Now, we solve for SD by finding the square root of the average of the deviations for the 10 true range cases we are examining as follows:

$$SD = \sqrt{\frac{\Sigma(X_{1-10} - \bar{X})^2}{10}}$$

which yields:

$$SD = \sqrt{\frac{.474}{9}} = .2296$$

The equation yields one standard deviation from the mean. Adding SD to the average and then adding it to the high (high + (SD + average)) and subtracting it from the low (low - (SD + average)) accounts for 68% of the variability we would normally expect in either direction of price movement. For the purposes of the opening-gap reversal entry, we are interested in two standard deviations, which accounts for 95% of the expected range of price. To accomplish this, we simply double the standard deviation. Next, add the doubled standard deviation to the mean. The result, 0.46, is now added to the high and subtracted from the low price of the stock. The resulting prices are the levels at which we will look to fade a gap the following morning. Then we have the following:

Lower gap reversal zone   30.91 - 0.46 = 30.45

Upper gap reversal zone   31.80 + 0.46 = 32.26

Table 12.2 shows the summary statistics for Urban Outfitters for the days considered here. These are easily derived, necessary to complete the gap computations and tell us a great deal about what is going on with the stock. Most analytical software will provide these descriptives, and it is always good practice to display them for the core group of stocks that you will be trading.

Descriptive statistics	
Mean	0.665
Standard error	0.072606244
Median	0.645
Standard deviation	0.229601103
Sample variance	0.052716667
Kurtosis	-1.737020127
Skewness	0.130021098
Range	0.62
Minimum	0.36
Maximum	0.98

TABLE 12.2 – URBAN OUTFITTERS DESCRIPTIVE STATISTICS

This completes the process of calculating the gap reversal zones for the opening-gap reversal pattern. Next we will look at the rules for pattern entry. Then we will examine the actual move in Urban Outfitters.

Once the calculations for the set-up are mastered and programmed, this is a simple pattern to find and trade. To make it work, you need to establish a means of finding morning gaps in either direction, establish 2.0 SD validity and then monitor for volume and price to indicate a reversal is in the making.

The ground rules are as follows:

1. A gap opening sends the price dramatically away from yesterday's close.

2. An interim support/resistance area forms at or beyond 2.0 standard deviations above the high, or below the low, of yesterday's range and the market fails to confirm the extension by way of volume.

3. We enter the trade just above the high (long trade) or below the low (short trade) of the last bar in the pullback. If the stock trades in a consolidation range before reversing, we enter on a breakout of the range.

4. The profit stop is executed at either the reversal of a profitable close on a five-minute chart, a violation of support or resistance on a 25-tick chart, a reversal of two closes on a three-minute chart or at a 38.2% retracement of a larger move.

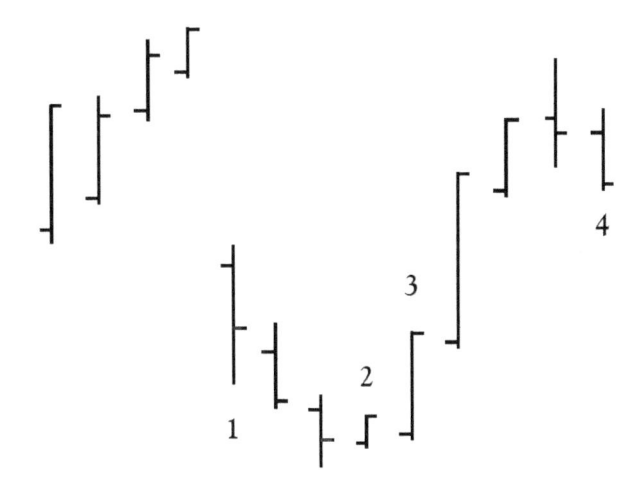

FIGURE 12.1

Urban Outfitters (URBN) reported second quarter results after the closing bell on 20 August 2012. The company's EPS was $0.42 versus consensus estimates of $0.33. Analysts at Wells Fargo, JP Morgan, and Baird immediately upgraded the stock and set the stage for a 21 August 2012 gap move higher. As we saw earlier, the stock would have to gap open to $32.26 in order to make a 2SD move in the morning. URBN made a much larger move, and quick profits by shorting the stock were easy around the open of trading.

1. URBN opens for trading at $36.91, more than $4 beyond the required gap at $32.26. The stock trades wildly for the first five minutes of the session before settling lower. The close of the first five-minute bar in the bottom of the range is indicative of an opportunity to short in the next few minutes.

2. The stock triggers a short-sale entry at $36.52 and trades as low as $36.06.

3. The trade is covered when the price violates the close of the previous five-minute bar at $36.22.

4. When price again violates the set-up bar low (1), another short-sale entry is triggered at $36.52.

5. URBN trades as low as $35.91 but finds support once again.

6. The trade is covered at $36.05 after the a violation of the previous bar's (5) closing price.

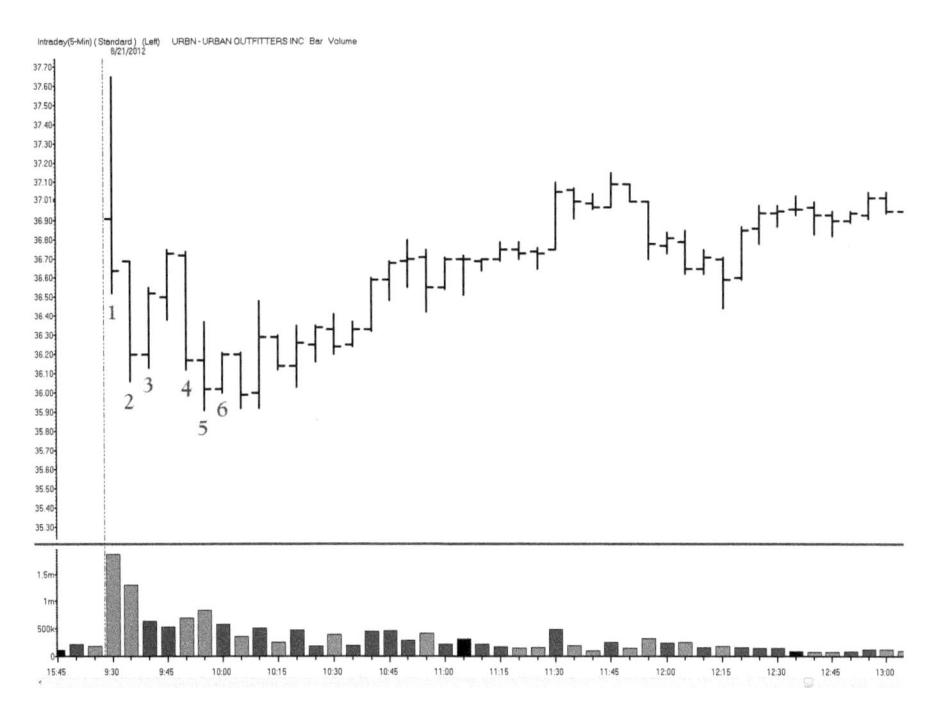

FIGURE 12.2 – URBAN OUTFITTERS
RealTick by Townsend Analytics, Ltd.

Aetna Inc. (AET) reported weaker-than-expected results before the open of trading on 26 April 2012. The stock had been trading in a narrow range and had a small SD value of .15 (see Table 12.3). This meant that a gap of just $0.30 (2 × .15) would represent a 2SD excursion from the mean. While a gap of just $0.30 does meet the technical requirements of the set-up, the spirit of the pattern is to identify larger moves. When AET gapped lower by $3.48, a good opportunity for an opening-gap reversal trade was evident.

Descriptive statistics	
Mean	0.764
Standard error	0.048630123
Median	0.725
Standard deviation	0.153781952
Sample variance	0.023648889
Kurtosis	-1.664149715
Skewness	0.412884432
Range	0.40
Minimum	0.61
Maximum	1.01

TABLE 12.3 – AETNA INC.

1. AET gaps lower after missing consensus earnings numbers.

2. The interim daily low of $43.35 is reached on heavy trading volume.

3. The deepest high of any five-minute bar of the session provides a potential entry on a reversal that trades above $43.84.

4. A long entry is triggered and AET trades as high as 44.31.

5. AET is sold when price violates the $44.30 close of the previous bar (4).

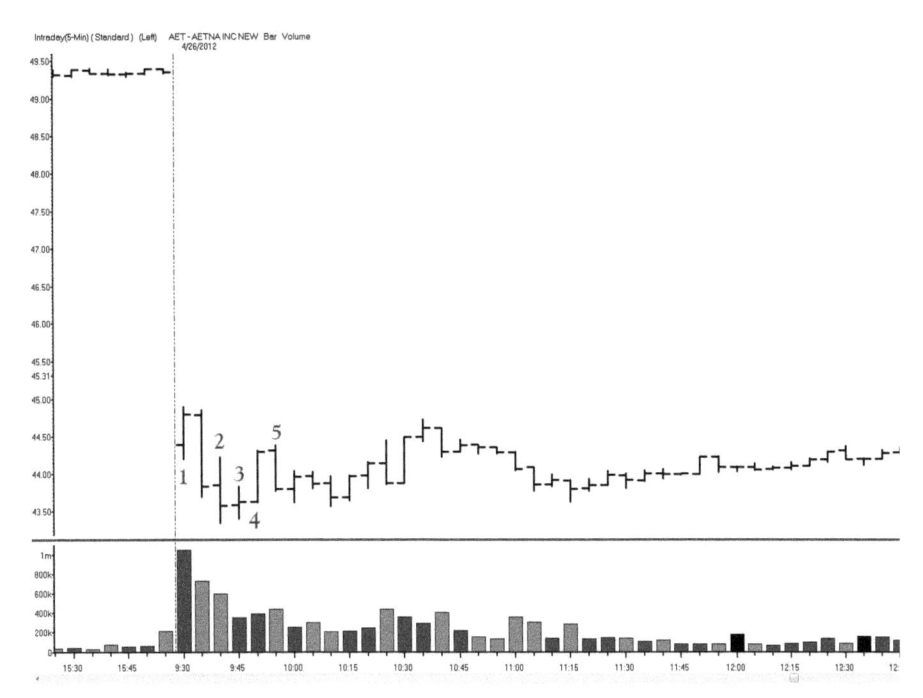

FIGURE 12.3 – AETNA INC.
RealTick by Townsend Analytics, Ltd.

An analyst upgrade for American Water Works (AWK) set up an opening-gap reversal on 3 August 2012. The stock generally trades in a narrow range, and a move of just $0.40 represents a 2SD gap.

Descriptive statistics	
Mean	0.626
Standard error	0.062275374
Median	0.565
Standard deviation	0.196932024
Sample variance	0.038782222
Kurtosis	-1.648180861
Skewness	0.324662846
Range	0.55
Minimum	0.38
Maximum	0.93

TABLE 12.4 – AMERICAN WATER WORKS INC.

1. A post-upgrade $1.08 gap higher sets up a potential short-sale entry in AWK.

2. A violation of the $37.42 low of the previous five-minute bar (1) triggers an entry.

3. The trade is covered when the $36.74 close of the prior low bar (A) is violated.

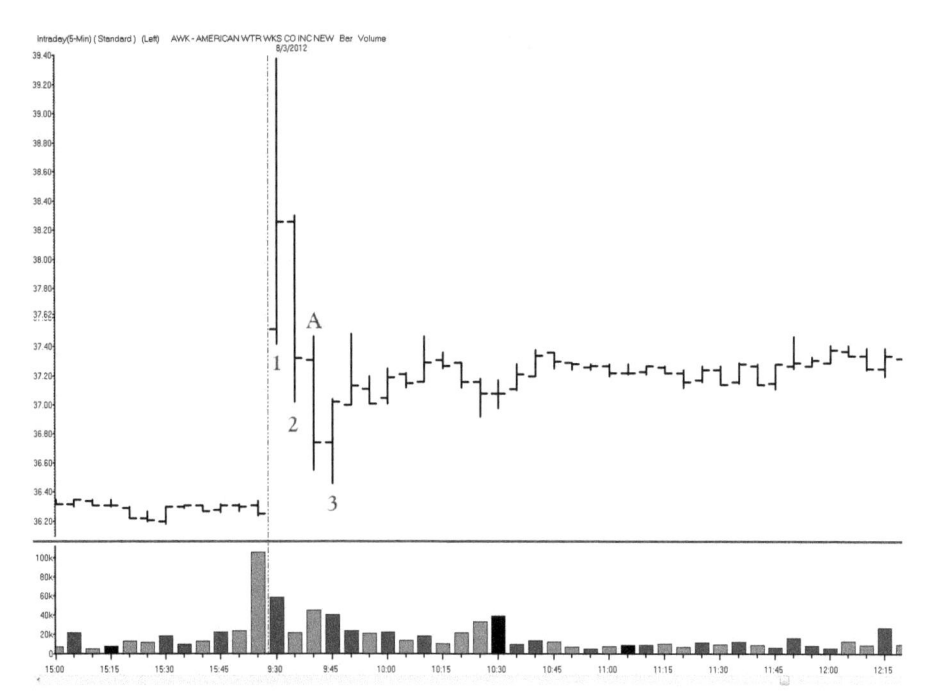

FIGURE 12.4 – AMERICAN WATER WORKS INC.
RealTick by Townsend Analytics, Ltd.

12. Opening-Gap Reversals | **111**

By mid-summer 2012 it was evident that retailer Best Buy (BBY) was in serious trouble. The company expected to meet its domestic share goal for the remainder of the year but had several negative factors to overcome, including a shake-up in management and the continued threat posed by internet retailers offering significantly lower prices. This led the company to announce that it would suspend future earnings guidance prior to the open of trading on 21 August 2012. This news had the stock indicated for a lower opening at the NYSE. A gap lower of $1.12 would represent a 2SD move and qualify for a potential opening-gap reversal trade.

Descriptive statistics	
Mean	0.884
Standard error	0.176837653
Median	0.62
Standard deviation	0.55920976
Sample variance	0.312715556
Kurtosis	1.661345435
Skewness	1.540678034
Range	1.67
Minimum	0.46
Maximum	2.13

TABLE 12.5 – BEST BUY

1. The stock gaps down by $2.82 and qualifies as an opening-gap-reversal set-up.

2. An inside bar forms and represents the deepest high. The trade will trigger in the next bar (2) if price exceeds the current $16.69 high.

3. An entry triggers above the $16.69 high, and BBY closes at $17.05.

4. After a failed attempt to push higher, the trade is closed when the $17.05 close (3) is violated.

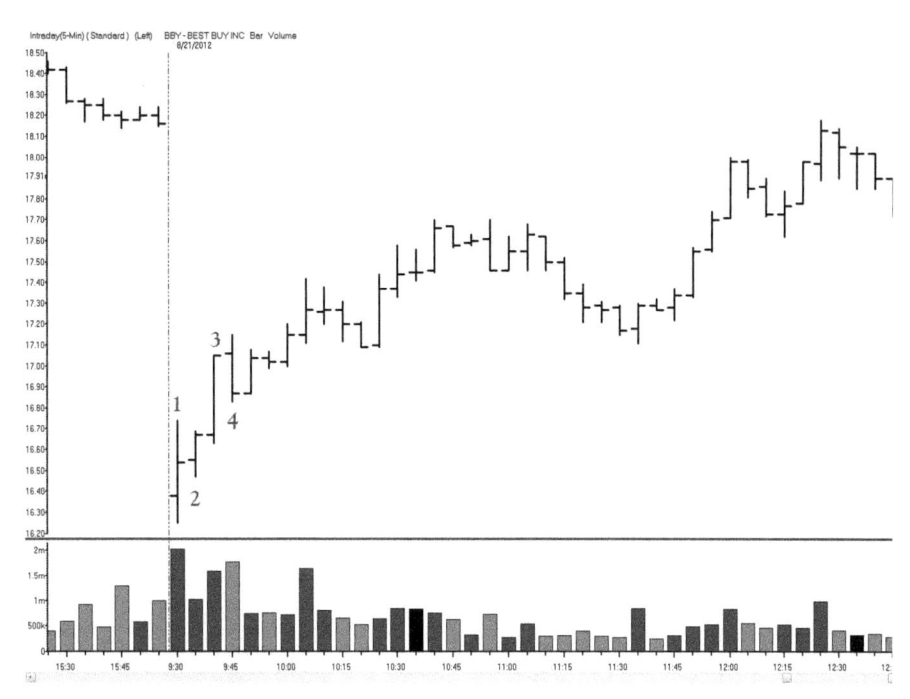

FIGURE 12.5 – BEST BUY
RealTick by Townsend Analytics, Ltd.

12. Opening-Gap Reversals | **113**

Harris Corp. (HRS) seemed to be on track for a solid year in April 2012. The company announced several large new contracts and better-than-expected results. Analysts did not like something they saw, however, and downgrades were released prior to the start of trading on 1 May. A $0.59 gap in either direction would represent a potential trading opportunity, so when the stock gapped $1.25 an opening-gap reversal was in the works.

Descriptive statistics	
Mean	0.722
Standard error	0.093900657
Median	0.64
Standard deviation	0.296939949
Sample variance	0.088173333
Kurtosis	0.356664927
Skewness	1.136483957
Range	0.88
Minimum	0.44
Maximum	1.32

TABLE 12.6 – HARRIS CORP.

1. HRS gaps lower by more than the 2SD threshold. The first bar of the day closes in the top of the range, making it likely that the second bar will be the trigger.

2. A violation of the high of the first bar at $44.11 initiates a long trade.

3. A $44.45 exit as the close of the entry bar (2) is violated.

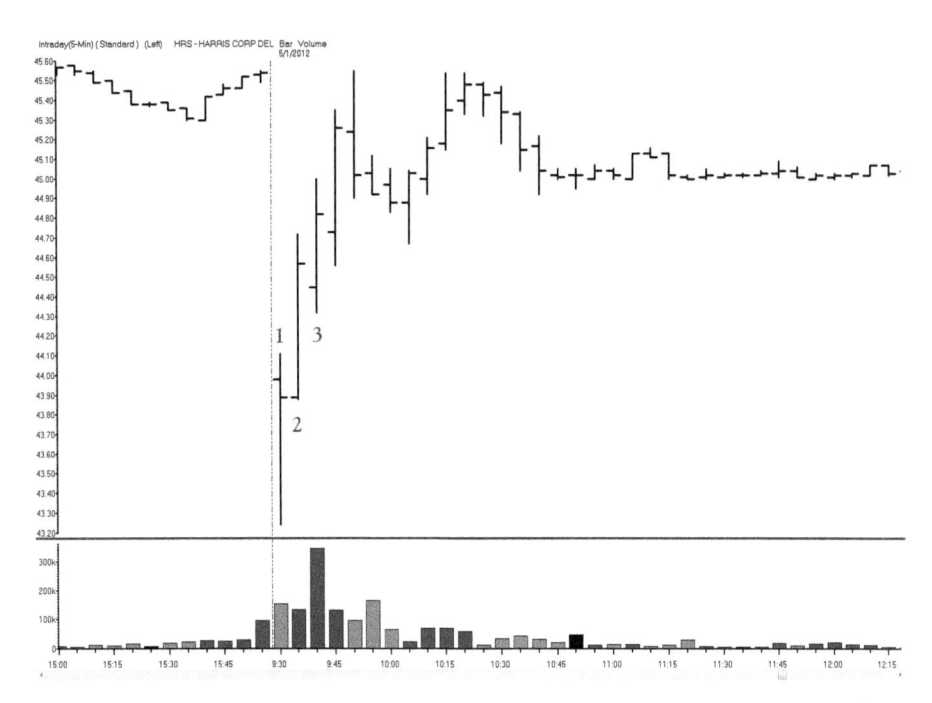

FIGURE 12.6 – HARRIS CORP.
RealTick by Townsend Analytics, Ltd.

12. Opening-Gap Reversals | **115**

Western Digital Corp. (WDC) was another 2012 downgrade victim. In April, the stock gapped lower by $4.51, well in excess of the $1.25 required for a 2SD move.

Descriptive statistics	
Mean	1.338
Standard error	0.196981669
Median	1.13
Standard deviation	0.62291073
Sample variance	0.388017778
Kurtosis	0.307511918
Skewness	1.214809001
Range	1.76
Minimum	0.8
Maximum	2.56

TABLE 12.7 – WESTERN DIGITAL CORP.

1. WDC gaps lower from a $44.10 close and opens at $38.80.

2. The stock continues to drop for three bars; each time a lower high is made, the potential entry price is lowered to the high of that bar. A tick above $37.74 is the entry threshold based on the current bar's high.

3. An entry triggers and WDC begins moving higher. Upon the close of the five-minute bar, the profit-protecting stop is moved to $38.05.

4. An additional profit extension raises the stop to $38.90.

5. The trailing stop triggers and the WDC trade is closed.

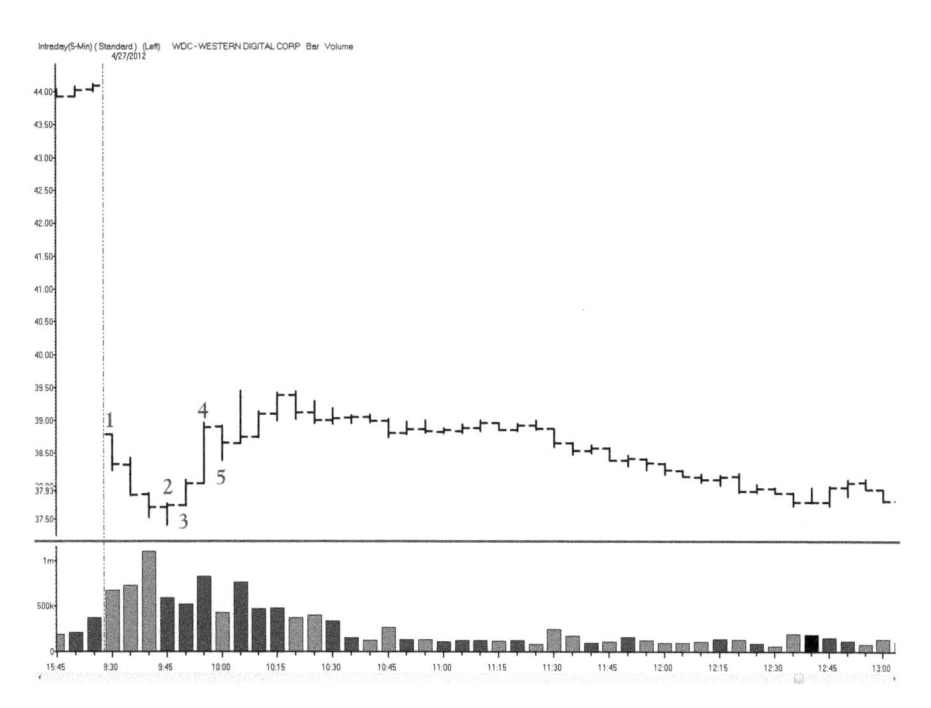

FIGURE 12.7 – WESTERN DIGITAL CORP.
RealTick by Townsend Analytics, Ltd.

Summary

The opening-gap reversal is a common pattern that occurs repeatedly on an almost daily basis. Once a trader is used to seeing the simple variations of the move it becomes progressively easier to separate the good ones from the bad. Since most direct-access trading software has provision for finding gaps, it is just a matter of flipping charts to find the ones that are running into resistance and have the potential to make for a good fade.

CHAPTER 13.
Consolidation Breaks

THE CONSOLIDATION-BREAK pattern solves a problem that plagued me early in my trading career. The issue had to do with spotting intraday set-ups and getting into positions when a stock seemed to be running away from me. Too often, my entry would be the extreme tick of the day; and I would watch in disgust as everything turned around and moved against me. The dilemma with a quick intraday move is always whether to try boarding a moving train, or to wait and see if it is going to stop at the station. Too often, the outcome of jumping in the middle of a trend is whiplash as price reverses and sends the stock immediately toward the stop loss. The solution for me was to wait for the move to consolidate at the extreme of the initial range, and then take an entry in the direction of the move only if a break from the consolidation reasserted the initial trend.

The consolidation-break pattern is very simple to spot. I use a five-minute chart and start flipping a symbol list comprised of stocks trading above (longs) or below (shorts) their 20, 50, and 200 simple moving average, with good ADX and DMI. I begin this process as soon as the market opens, and keep a scribbled list of everything that is moving in concert with my primary criteria.

The pattern can actually occur at any time during the day, but I like it best right off the open. The rules for longs and shorts are as follows:

1. The stock must make a large-range five-minute move higher or lower.

2. The price consolidates in a narrow range with clearly identifiable highs and lows for at least three bars.

3. Entry is on a .05 to .10 break that clearly violates the consolidation. The stop is the opposite extreme of the consolidation range.

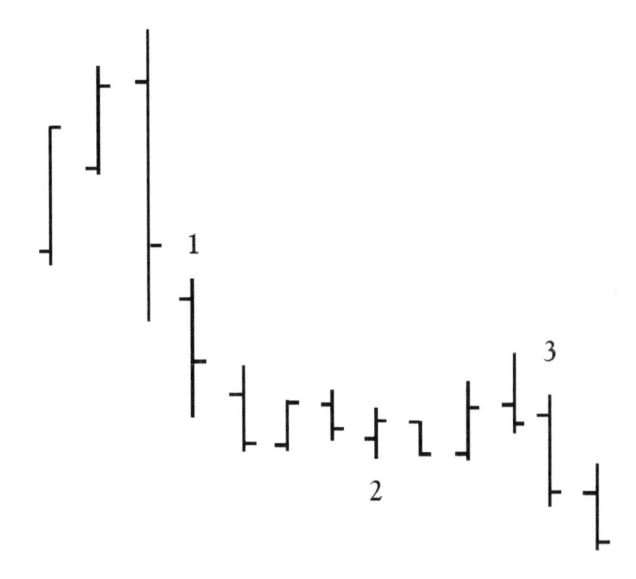

FIGURE 13.1

13. Consolidation Breaks | **119**

Kinder Morgan Energy Partners Ltd. (KMP) made a mid-summer high in mid-July 2012 and began moving lower. A wide-range opening bar in this volatile stock set the stage for a good consolidation breakdown entry opportunity.

1. A gap lower in KMP is followed by volatile trading in the first five minutes of the session on 27 July 2012.

2. KMP trades in a tight consolidation range for 30 minutes.

3. A consolidation breakdown triggers an $81.75 short-sale entry.

4. The stock makes a $0.65 move lower.

5. A reversal of two-closing prices triggers a $81.20 exit.

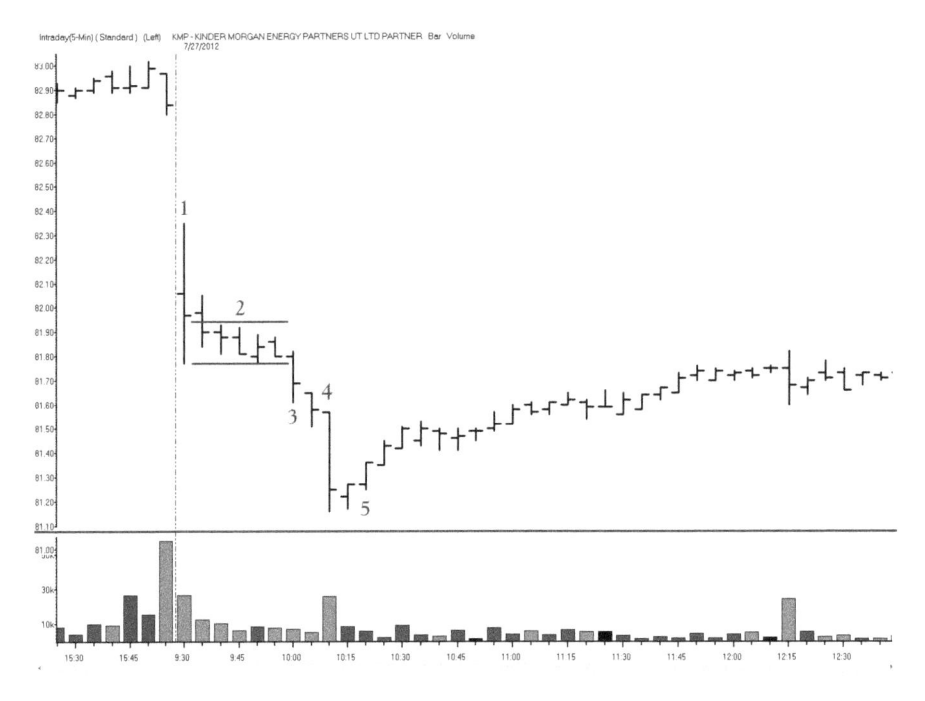

FIGURE 13.2 – KINDER MORGAN ENERGY PARTNERS LTD.
RealTick by Townsend Analytics, Ltd.

Consolidation breaks frequently occur at the open, but they are equally valid set-ups when they happen later in the day. This example in Sonic Automotive Inc. (SAH) started during the noon hour, and broke higher nearly 90 minutes later.

1. SAH made a wide-range move higher on 17 July 2012.

2. The stock made a lunch-session consolidation that lasted well into the afternoon.

3. After low-volume midday trading, the stock moves through the top of the range and triggers an entry at $15.50.

4. The move in SAH yields a $0.30 per share gain and triggers an exit on a reversal of two closing prices.

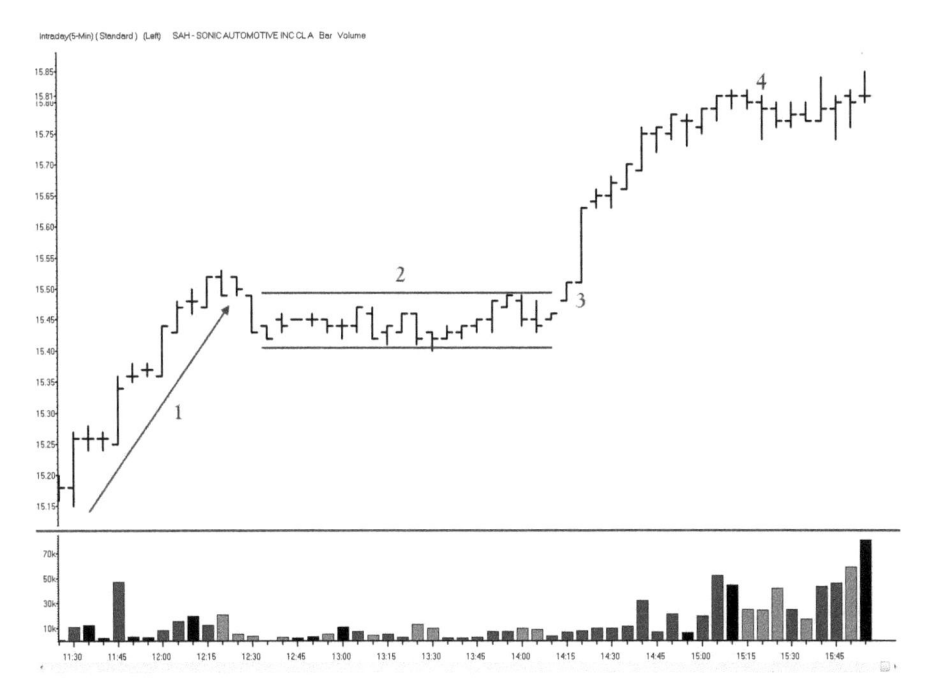

FIGURE 13.3 – SONIC AUTOMOTIVE INC.
RealTick by Townsend Analytics, Ltd.

13. Consolidation Breaks | 121

FMC Technologies (FTI) makes frequent intraday consolidation breaks. I keep the stock on a watch list that I flip through over the course of the day. Whenever a sideways move starts I look for trading opportunities on a break from the channel. Not every entry is a big winner, but staying vigilant pays off over the long run.

1. A wide range move higher on low volume is followed by a retracement.
2. A consolidation range forms with easily identifiable extremes.
3. A consolidation breakout triggers an entry.
4. FTI trades higher, but closes the five-minute bar on sell-side volume.
5. An intraday kings-and-queens reversal indicates that a move back into the channel is in the making.
6. An exit is triggered for a small loss as the stock moves through the top parallel of the channel and violates a support stop.
7. Another entry opportunity triggers as FTI reverses higher and violates the top of the range again.
8. A small profit is realised when a reversal of two closes triggers a quick exit.

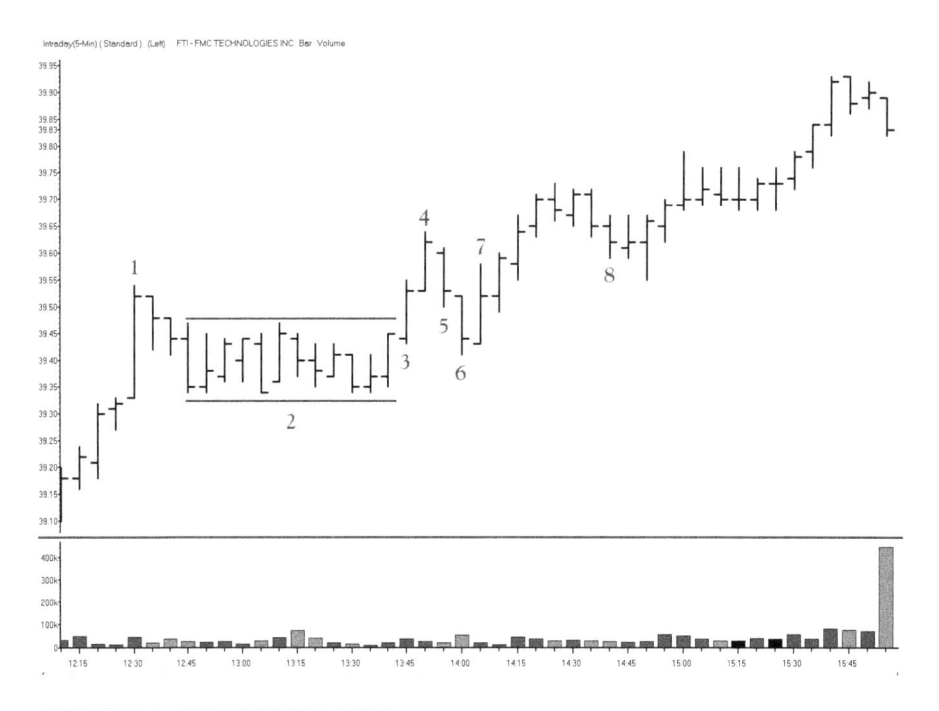

FIGURE 13.4 – FMC TECHNOLOGIES
RealTick by Townsend Analytics, Ltd.

Another FTI trade demonstrates why I like to follow a core list of stocks every day. This one occurred two weeks after the previous example.

1. FTI makes a wide-range opening move.

2. A short but well-defined consolidation range forms.

3. A break lower moves the stock marginally in my favour. The trailing stop shall remain a violation of the lower parallel.

4. FTI retraces to the low of the bar that created the breakdown entry; a secondary consolidation seems to be forming.

5. A break below the secondary consolidation lows, and FTI moves a total of $0.50 in favour of the short sale before triggering an intraday kings-and-queens reversal exit.

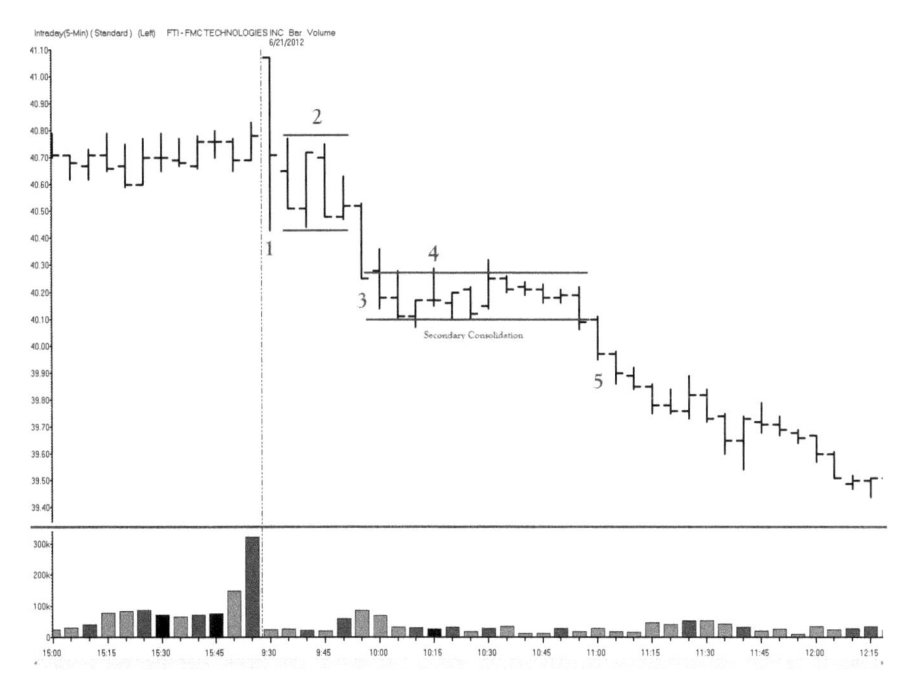

FIGURE 13.5 – FMC TECHNOLOGIES
RealTick by Townsend Analytics, Ltd.

13. Consolidation Breaks | **123**

Consolidation breakouts and breakdowns do not always work out on the first thrust. It is fairly common for the volume-weighted average price of the consolidation range to act like a magnet, pulling price back inside and adding to the duration of the consolidation. When this happens, I look for five-minute support and resistance to provide me with a money-management strategy.

1. Cameron International Corp. (CAM) makes a wide-range opening move in the first five minutes of trading on 25 June 2012. The stock is selling off after analysts lowered earnings estimates for the oil and gas group.

2. A sideways consolidation forms; the upper and lower channel lines are used as breakout or breakdown trigger zones.

3. A breakdown moves the stock $0.20 below the bottom of the consolidation.

4. CAM reverses and stops at the most recent consolidation lows, just a few pennies shy of triggering a stop loss.

5. After failing to move back into the consolidation range, the stock retests the low break (2).

6. Volume increases as the stock begins to deepen its sell-off.

7. Another consolidation range forms; there is no reason to exit the trade. Later in the session, the position is closed for a $0.60 profit on the short sale.

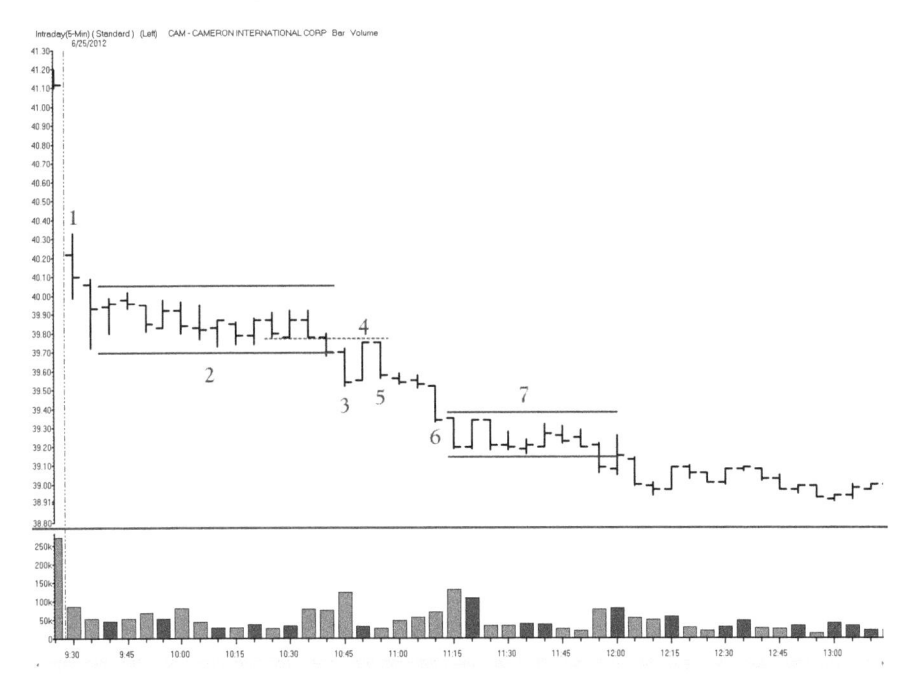

FIGURE 13.6 – CAMERON INTERNATIONAL CORP.
RealTick by Townsend Analytics, Ltd.

When the FDA approved a neuropathy therapy submitted by Baxter Pharmaceuticals Inc. (BAX), the company's stock was positioned for a move higher. But when a planned gap-extension entry gapped beyond the allowable slippage, a consolidation breakout provided a second chance to get a long entry.

1. A gap open has the stock trading beyond the planned gap extension entry.

2. BAX trades in a consolidation range with a tightening bias toward an upside breakout as the range develops.

3. The stock triggers an entry at $52.55 and begins travelling higher.

4. Over the course of the day, BAX drifts higher through two additional consolidations (A, B) without a significant reversal, closing at $53.16.

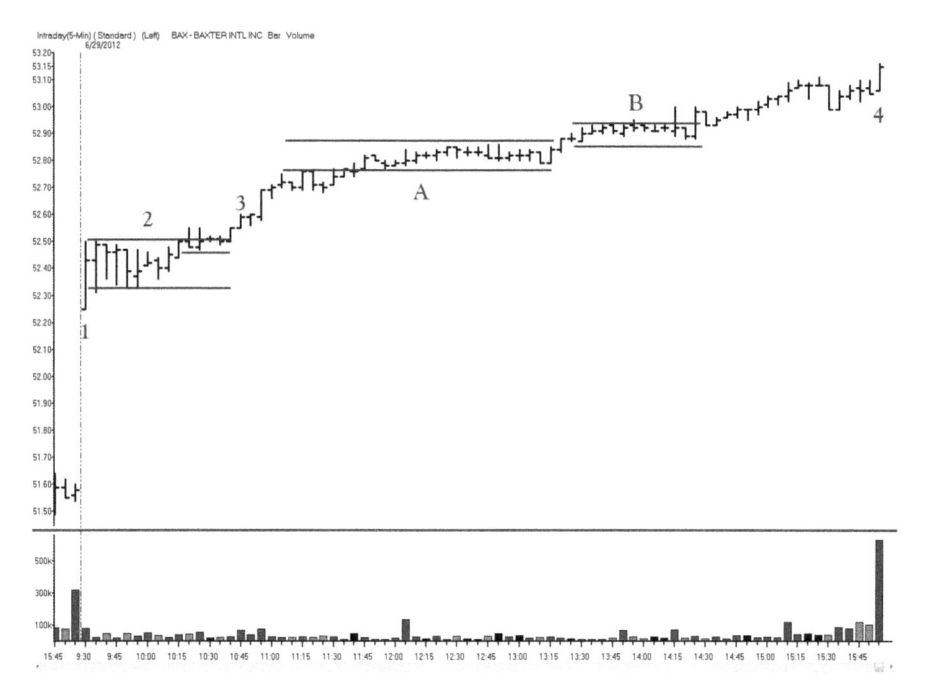

FIGURE 13.7 – BAXTER PHARMACEUTICALS INC.
RealTick by Townsend Analytics, Ltd.

Stocks traded on NASDAQ tend to have a bit more price elasticity at support and resistance levels than their NYSE counterparts, but there are still a few that I really like to trade. Monster Beverage (MNST), which we first came across in Chapter 11, is one such stock. It has very good intraday range and provides lots of trading opportunities. First breakouts with MNST, however, frequently lead to quick exits and re-entries.

1. MNST makes an intraday range move above current resistance.

2. The stock settles into a consolidation range with previous resistance defining the bottom of the channel.

3. A breakout of the top of the channel triggers an entry.

4. MNST reverses back into the channel and triggers an exit for a small loss.

5. A second breakout triggers a second entry and pushes price higher.

6. The trade is closed at the end of the day for a $0.50-per-share profit.

FIGURE 13.8 – MONSTER BEVERAGE CORP.
RealTick by Townsend Analytics, Ltd.

126 | Beat the Street

Summary

When it comes to trading, simpler is usually better. The consolidation break is about as simple as a pattern gets. What this pattern lacks in sophistication, it makes up for in reliability; and I will take the latter over the former any day. The key here is spotting the opportunities when they exist. The best means of accomplishing this is to develop a discipline of flipping through a list of stocks matching narrowly defined criteria and pulling only those set-ups that are perfect. Much like any entry, if you try to force something that is not there, the result will more likely be burnt fingers than profitability.

CHAPTER 14.
Momentum Reversals

WHEN AN expansion-of-range-and-volume trade sets up, sometimes the market response is to pass on the previous day's momentum and let the stock retrace a portion of the expansion move. The momentum reversal gives us an intraday entry opportunity just when we would have otherwise thought that a pattern was going to fail to hand us profits.

Pattern failures are a disappointing fact of a trader's life. In the case of a failed expansion-of-range-and-volume set-up, however, they can be the seeds of opportunity. The momentum reversal relies on the propensity of wide range days to be followed by additional volatility, even if the result is not follow-through. Basically, the trade is a means of anticipating the fear of traders who caught the tail-end of the prior day's move and now feel that it is time to quickly head for the exit.

The criteria for longs and shorts are as follows:

1. The stock opens and trades in the direction of the previous day's range expansion high or low.

2. The expansion-of-range-and-volume pattern fails to break out, or breaks out and reverses. The stock then trades in a short consolidation shy of the previous day's range extreme.

3. Entry is a few ticks outside the consolidation range.

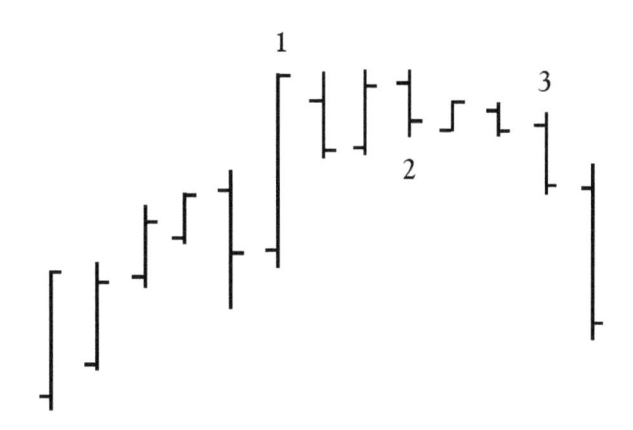

FIGURE 14.1

An expansion-of-range-and-volume set-up in Kinder Morgan Energy Partners Ltd (KMP), on 19 July 2012, looked as though it might offer terrific follow-through the next day. KMP had announced a long-term partnership with BP, and the commitment of 40,000 barrels per day of throughput seemed to be a very good commercial agreement for the company. But the excitement over the deal quickly faded, and there was no expansion-of-range-and-volume breakout on the day that the trade was planned. That did not mean, however, that there was not an opportunity for profit.

1. KMP attempts to push higher, but consolidates below the trigger price.

2. Low volume during the consolidation range is coupled with a price bias toward the low side of the channel.

3. A break through the channel low provides an opportunity for a countertrend short-sale entry.

4. The stock makes a wide range, $0.35 per-share move lower over the next hour of trading.

5. An ascending triangle resolves with a fractional move higher.

6. A new consolidation range forms, and KMP trades within narrow parallels for most of the remainder of the session.

7. A consolidation breakdown entry triggers as KMP begins selling off into the final 20 minutes of the session.

8. KMP adds $0.40 in profits, closing the day with a heavy-volume sell-off.

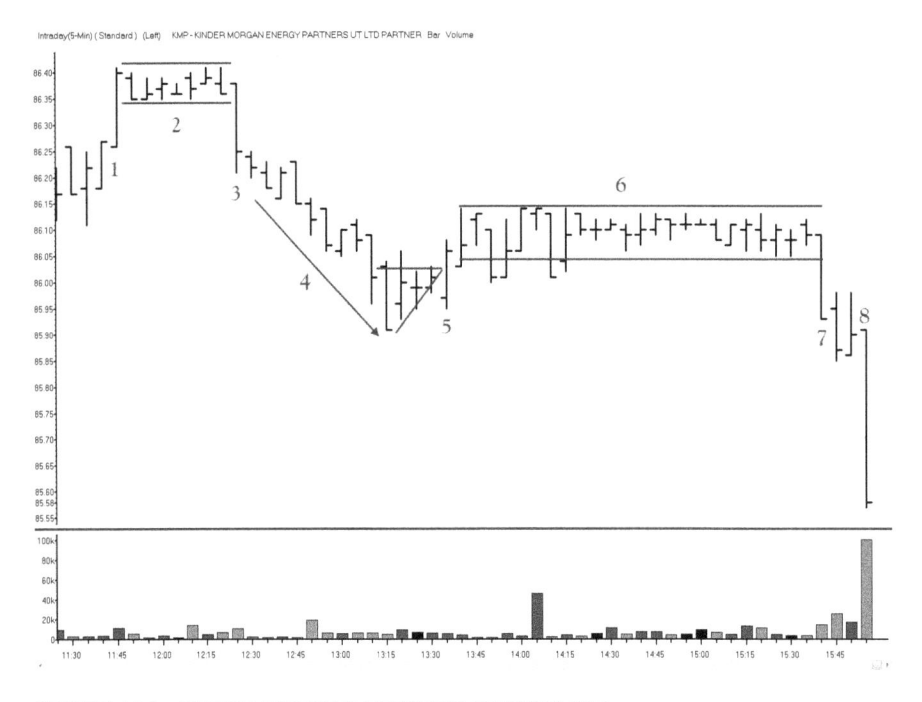

FIGURE 14.2 – KINDER MORGAN ENERGY PARTNERS LTD.
RealTick by Townsend Analytics, Ltd.

Target Stores (TGT) was an expansion-of-range-and-volume candidate for the trading session of 11 June 2012. However, prior to the opening bell, the company announced a change in its dividend; and that was almost certain to affect trading during the session. While this is not the easiest example to trade, it does shed light on the types of low-level set-ups that can generate substantial profits over time.

1. An attempted breakout of the high of 10 June 2012 fails to push TGT higher.
2. A three-bar consolidation has the stock's price right at the previous session's close. This is almost certainly a decision point for many traders who bought the stock on the expansion-of-range-and-volume day, hoping for a move higher.
3. A quick pop below the low of the consolidation triggers a short sale.
4. After stopping out on a move back into the previous consolidation, shares of TGT are, once again, trading in the previous day's closing range. The short consolidation shows a downwardly sloping bias, indicating again that a move lower may be in the making.
5. A short sale is triggered as TGT trades down through the bottom of the channel.
6. A substantial intraday consolidation forms on the five-minute chart.
7. A consolidation breakdown triggers as TGT moves below the lower band of the range.
8. The entry (5) results in a $0.40-per-share profit by the end of trading.

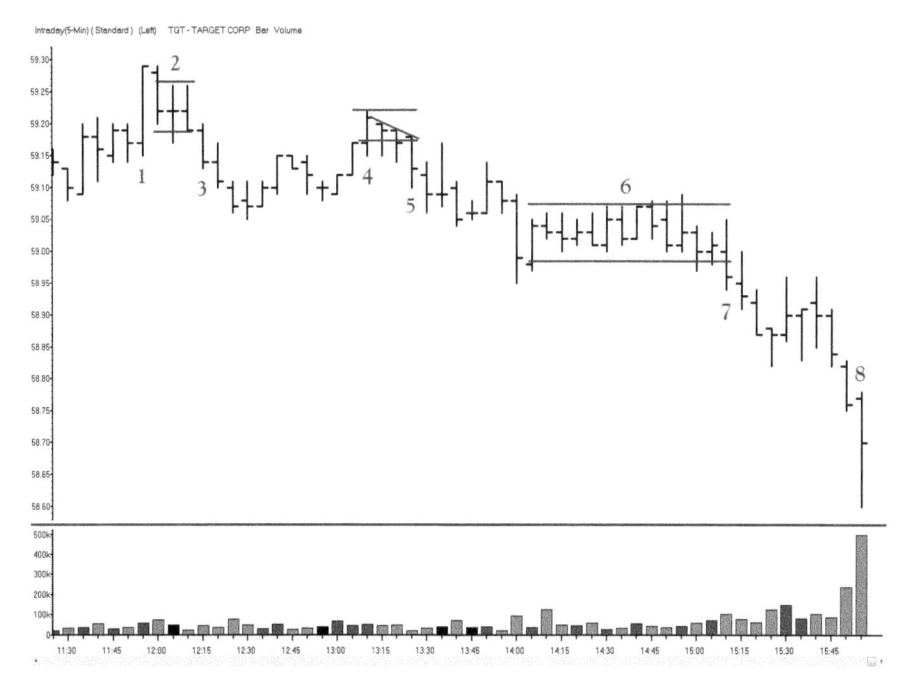

FIGURE 14.3 – TARGET STORES
RealTick by Townsend Analytics, Ltd.

14. Momentum Reversals | **131**

No news was definitely not good news for an expansion-of-range-and-volume set-up in Procter & Gamble (PG) on 8 June 2012. The trades in PG do make for an excellent example of what to look for when trying to spot opportunities intraday.

1. An attempted long-side breakout fails to follow through when PG meets pivot resistance in early trading. Pivot lines are definite points of inflection during the day, and a failure to penetrate is often, but not always, an indication that a stock will reverse course.

2. The stock trades in a symmetrical triangle that begins to consolidate just above the expansion-of-range-and-volume high.

3. A push lower to $62.89 still has the stock net positive on the session, and buying is sparked when PG nearly touches the high of the last session. There are always traders who buy dips, and an expansion-of-range-and-volume set-up shall definitely have many people eager to test the set-up on any pullback. The reversal forms an intraday kings-and-queens pattern.

4. PG meets supply again at the top of the previous range (2).

5. The previous area of supply (2) once again acts to push the stock lower through the bottom of the channel. PG enters a consolidation range enveloping the expansion-of-range-and-volume day's closing price. A momentum reversal appears to be setting up on a break down below the low of the A–B channel.

6. PG triggers a short sale on a violation of the lower parallel (B).

7. Another support level is easily identified when PG trades at support from the previous session. The stock had moved lower from this level about an hour before the expansion-of-range-and-volume session close, so it warrants staying with the trade as PG tests the price elasticity of the support.

8. A failure to continue lower results in price moving back above the support level (7). Based on the expansion-of-range-and-volume day price action, this is a signal to exit the trade before upside momentum reasserts itself. The profit on the set-up is fractional, but the trade does a nice job of illustrating the logic involved in intraday decision-making.

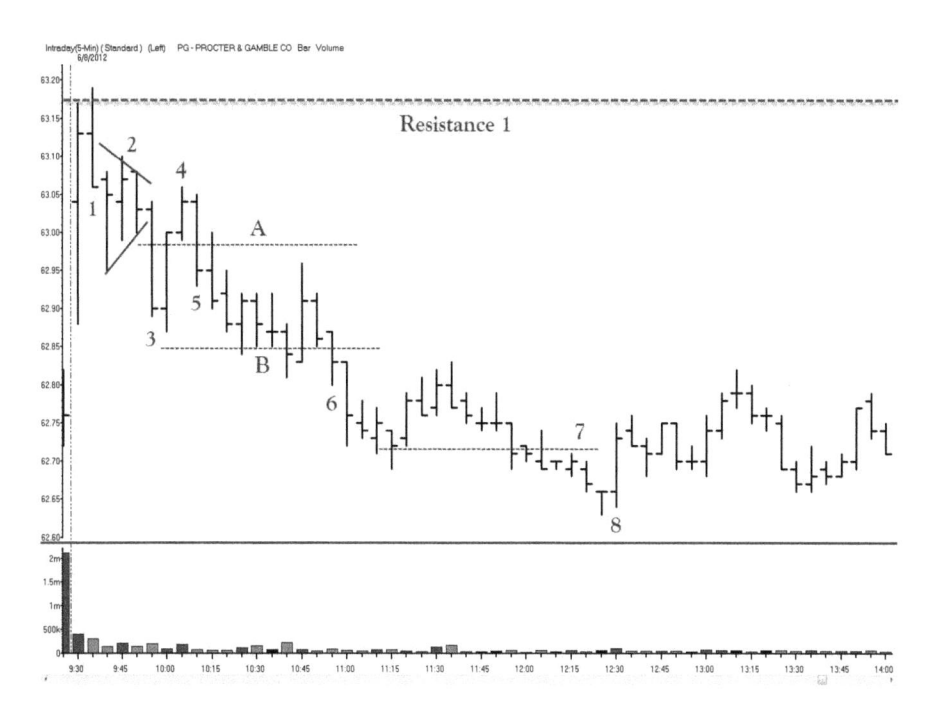

FIGURE 14.4 – PROCTER & GAMBLE
RealTick by Townsend Analytics, Ltd.

14. Momentum Reversals | **133**

An analyst upgrade in late February 2012 triggered a gap extension in Domino's Pizza (DPZ). Initially it looked as though the gap would move the stock out of its flat trading range and propel shares significantly higher, but within a few weeks, it became evident that DPZ was trading in an island top. The stock gapped lower on 22 March, 2012, and started a distribution-phase consolidation channel right on top of its previous range-bound trading zone. Distribution phases are followed by mark-down phases, and DPZ began to slide in late April, offering trading opportunities well into the summer. An expansion-of-range-and-volume short-sale failure on 18 May offered opportunities for profits in the direction of the originally planned trade, even as the stock violated the set-up twice.

1. An expansion-of-range-and-volume in DPZ triggers and reverses. The trade stops out for a loss (A) and continues higher.

2. DPZ breaks through the central pivot and begins a symmetrical triangle consolidation.

3. When the apex of the triangle and channel support are violated, a short sale is initiated at $30.75.

4. A secondary consolidation forms just above the previous session's closing range.

5. After attempting to move higher, DPZ reverses again and breaks through support at the bottom of the channel.

6. An intraday ratio pullback retraces some of the morning's decline and then resolves with another move lower.

7. When the stock reaches the expansion-of-range-and-volume entry price again, support once more is evident. The bounce of the previous intraday low is the signal to close the trade for a gain of $0.75 per share.

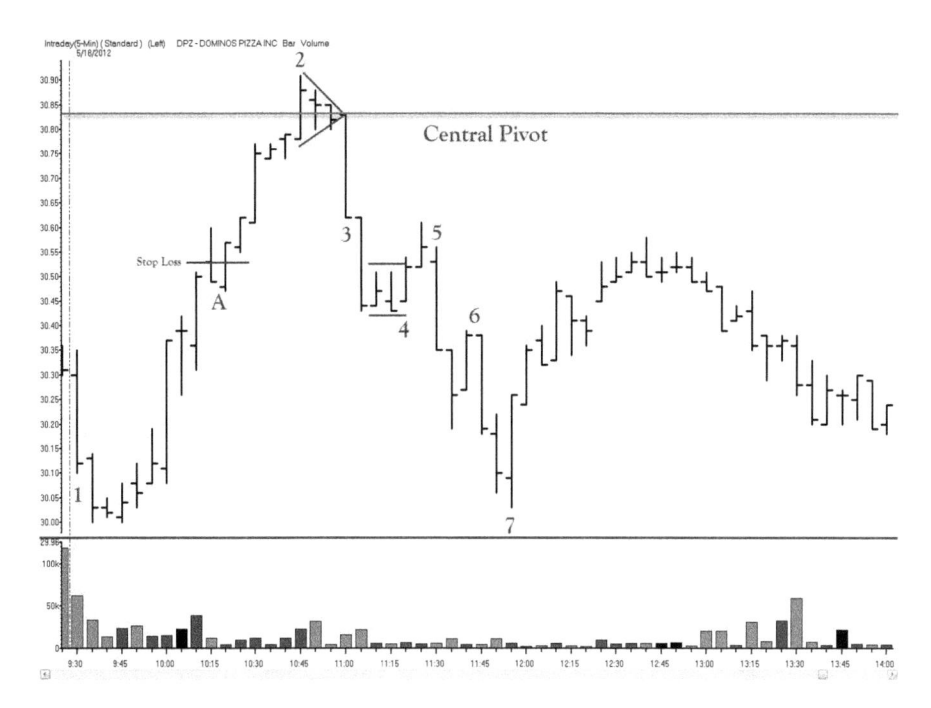

FIGURE 14.5 – DOMINO'S PIZZA
RealTick by Townsend Analytics, Ltd.

Allergan Inc. (AGN) was an expansion-of-range-and-volume short sale on 18 May 2012. When the stock reversed higher and stopped out just above a consolidation range, it offered us an opportunity to reverse the position and save a commission in the process.

1. AGN opens and triggers a short sale.

2. The stock misses the 50%-to-target hurdle by $.07. If this level had been hit, my stop would have been moved to break-even. As of this low, however, the full stop at $89.17 is still in place.

3. AGN forms a consolidation just below the short-sale stop loss.

4. A breakout above the channel moves AGN to the stop loss. Because the move through the stop is also a momentum reversal trigger, I buy twice the number of shares that were shorted. This closes the short position and establishes a long position, while incurring only one commission for the trades.

5. AGN travels to the intraday resistance target at $89.70. This level represented intraday support during the expansion-of-range-and-volume-set-up day and was also just below the current session's central pivot.

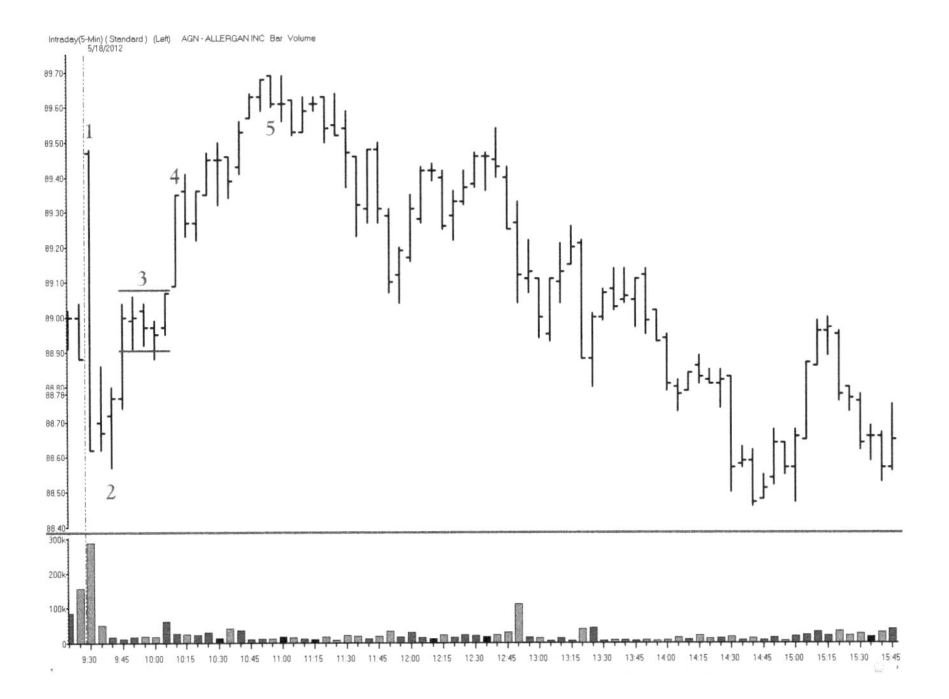

FIGURE 14.6 – ALLERGAN INC.
RealTick by Townsend Analytics, Ltd.

Lennar Corp. (LEN) was an expansion-of-range-and-volume long trade for 10 May 2012. A stop loss was the result of the first trade, but a momentum reversal set-up offered an entry on the short side of the market, and this led to a profitable position.

1. A failed expansion-of-range-and-volume breakout immediately forms an opening range consolidation in the form of an intraday kings-and-queens reversal. An entry is triggered on a violation of the lower parallel of the channel.

2. The short entry in LEN generates $0.90 per share in a smooth sell-off move during the first hour of trading. The stock forms a new consolidation range (A).

3. A move higher violates the high of the consolidation range (A) and triggers an exit. Since the stock is oscillating at the central pivot, no reversal trade is entered after the consolidation break set-up (A).

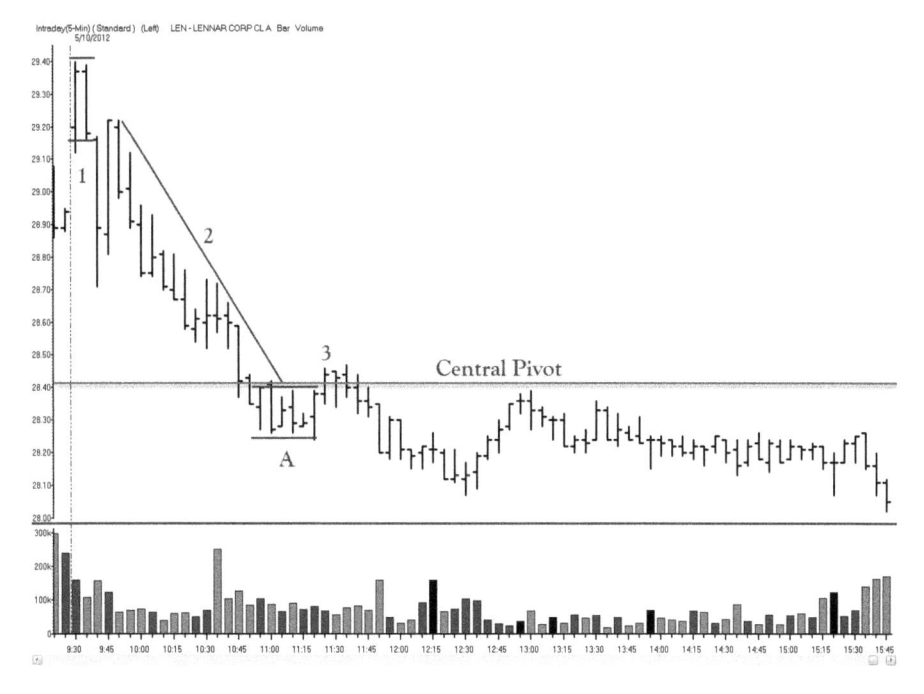

FIGURE 14.7 – LENNAR CORP.
RealTick by Townsend Analytics, Ltd.

Bunge Limited (BG) is a stock that appears on my trading plan very regularly. An expansion-of-range-and-volume set-up failed to trigger an entry, but the less-than-perfect set-up was intriguing enough to take two entries on the move lower.

1. BG makes two failed attempts to break higher and fails.

2. A break lower meets with intraday support from the expansion-of-range-and-volume session.

3. A low level consolidation forms inside the previous session's bar. The location of the consolidation is in line with substantial support from the previous day's opening range. Because of this, I treat the current consolidation as a valid set-up, even though the reversal has moved a bit further than I prefer.

4. A break through the bottom of the channel results in BG trading at the expansion-of-range-and-volume day's low. BG is also trading just below support 1.

5. A reversal through the pivot stops the trade out for a fractional gain.

6. The previous consolidation range (3) appears once again. Another short trade is planned. The target on a re-entry will be the low established earlier (4).

7. The break below the channel initiates a short sale in BG.

8. The trade attempts to break below the morning low (4) and reverses. The exit is at the level of the prior $68.68 low (4).

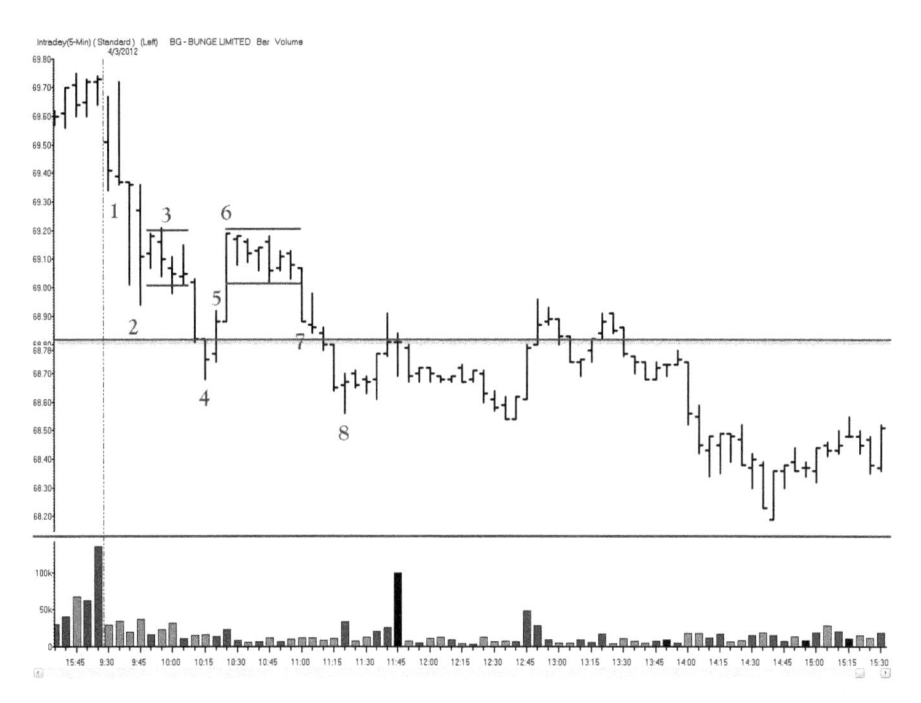

FIGURE 14.8 – BUNGE LIMITED
RealTick by Townsend Analytics, Ltd.

The momentum reversal gets us in a scoring position when other market factors seem to be working against our plan. Although I always advocate sticking to the pre-planned trades, this one can be anticipated the night before and kept aside as a contingency. On those occasions that it pans out, the pattern can provide quick profits with very limited risk.

CHAPTER 15. Keeping Score

Every trader benefits by knowing what happened, when it happened and why. The problem for most of us is that we focus on our results and not the chain of events that led to them. By the time we realise that there is a problem, the only way we can figure out the cause is to go back and attempt to reconstruct history with little working evidence to help us. This ends up being a speculative and largely fruitless exercise.

Contrast this with the practices of successful traders who have closets full of their log files for each and every trade. When something goes wrong, these people have an objective means of addressing the problem before it gets out of hand. When things go well, they can review their notes and create their daily plan with an emphasis on what works for them. In this chapter I will show you how to join their ranks, by introducing an effective means of logging every planned and executed trade.

Keeping an accurate record of every trade that is planned and every trade that triggers is a prerequisite for success. You can try to survive in this business without going through the hassle of logging everything, but if that's your intention, then you may as well just burn your money one note at a time. I assure you, it will last longer; and at least you will be entertained and warm instead of frustrated and sick to your stomach.

The temptation for most traders is to log the big winners, log the trades that blow out, and forget about everything else. This practice results in 90% of activity being lost forever. To say that something in this business is unimportant because it is mundane borders on the ridiculous. Trading is not the thrill of victory and the agony of defeat. It is about going to work and making money. It often revolves around doing nothing. During much of the trading day, our hands serve us best as seat cushions. This is a profession that requires acute attention and focus on the details. A highly descriptive trade log is part of success.

I run a nightly trading service for a small list of subscribers. I started this as much to keep focus and discipline as I did in response to requests from traders to share my stock selections. Every night I plan everything for the next trading session down to the last detail. I record entry triggers, logical profit targets, logical stop losses and all the anticipated areas of support and resistance that will be encountered during the day. I identify the sector with which each stock is most highly correlated and note the relative strength value associated with it. I keep my plans in three ring binders and review them religiously to make sure that there is continuity in my approach.

I also keep a log file of every trade. I take a snapshot of the intraday chart and post it in a log file template. I mark the entry, support and resistance encountered, and the exit. I then write a brief commentary of what happened once the trade triggered. I do this for every trade. Often this means chronicling events that are as mundane as "we entered at 50.20, and the trade drifted slowly to our stop loss." For me, this is not tedium but necessity.

On the following pages, you will find some actual examples from my service and log files.[1]

---

[1] The following examples contain excerpts from Tricks of the Trade Peterson/Manz Trading Trade Log 2012 © 2012 Peterson/Manz Trading, Inc. Past Results are not indicative of future returns. There is a high degree of risk in trading. Peterson/Manz Trading, Inc. assumes no responsibility for your trading results. Principals of Peterson/Manz Trading, Inc. may at times maintain, directly or indirectly, positions mentioned in this service.

Around The Horn Plan
Thursday, August 02, 2012

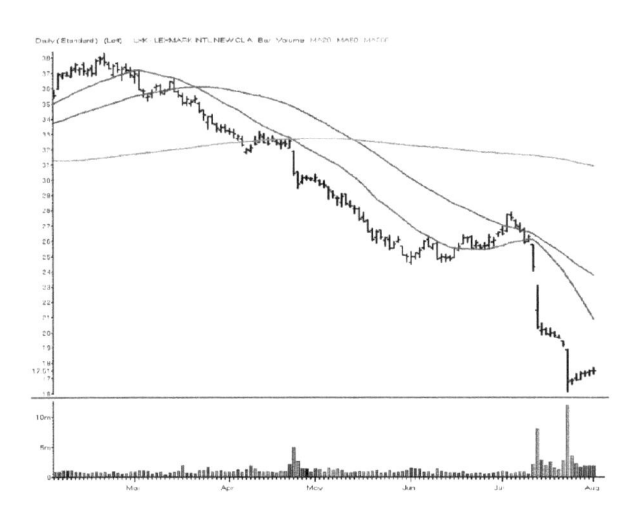

Symbol	LXK	Sector Symbol	$XIT.X
Description	LEXMARK INTL NEW CL A		
Pattern	Ratio Pullback	Computer Storage & Peripherals	

Position	Short	Resistance 2	17.96
Entry	17.16	Resistance 1	17.73
Stop	17.40	Pivot	17.50
Initial Target	16.80	Support 1	17.27
Ratio	1.50	Support 2	17.04
50% To Target	16.98		

FIGURE 15.1

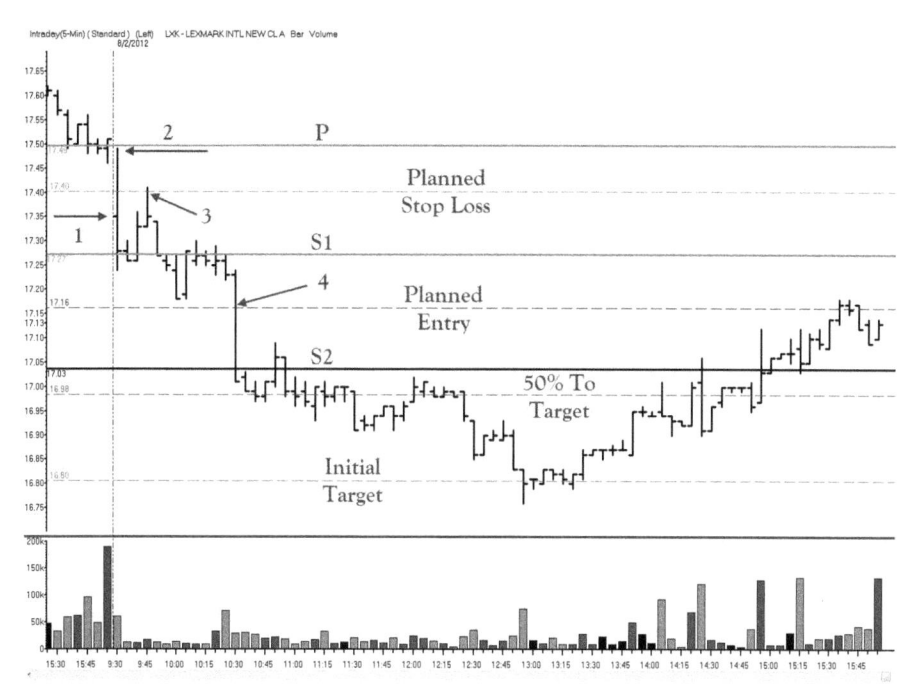

FIGURE 15.2 – LEXMARK
RealTick by Townsend Analytics, Ltd.

Lexmark (LXK) opened just below the planned support/resistance stop loss that I planned for the session. When the stock traded higher to closing resistance from the previous session, and was also trading just below the central pivot (P), I knew that there was an opportunity for an early entry. Trading that occurs right at two levels of resistance generally indicates that there will be a move lower. The overlap between the central pivot and the closing support from the set-up day gave me cause to short the stock well ahead of the planned entry. The $17.49 (2) early trade had a tight stop of $17.57, just above the previous closing support high, making this a very low risk entry. As long as the stock stayed net negative on the day, I planned to keep the early entry open.

LXK made a move lower to S1 and then tested the $17.40 stop loss posted in the trading plan. If I had not taken the earlier pivot entry, the resistance that asserted itself at the stop would have had me interested in opening a position at $17.39 with a stop at $17.45. LXK then retested S1 and oscillated for 40 minutes.

LXK moved lower, through the entry price, and I doubled my position with an entry per the parameters of the trading plan. When price moved lower to the 50%-

to-target level of $16.98, the stop for the entire position, including the early entry (2), was moved to $17.16. After consolidating below S2, LXK moved to the initial profit target and the position was closed. The target proved to be the low of the day, demonstrating the efficacy of the simple support/resistance method of developing targets.

Around The Horn Plan
Tuesday, August 07, 2012

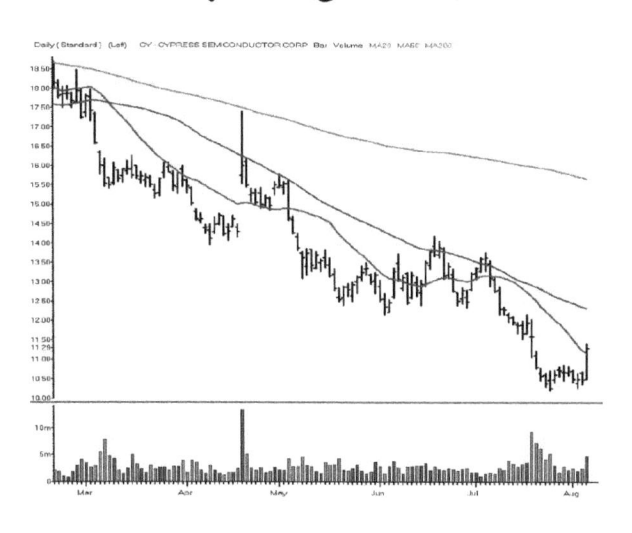

Symbol	CY	Sector Symbol	SSOX.X
Description	CYPRESS SEMICONDUCTOR CORP		
Pattern	XRV	Semiconductors	

Position	Long	Resistance 2	11.98
Entry	11.51	Resistance 1	11.64
Stop	11.19	Pivot	11.06
Initial Target	11.96	Support 1	10.72
Ratio	1.41	Support 2	10.14
50% To Target	11.74		

FIGURE 15.3

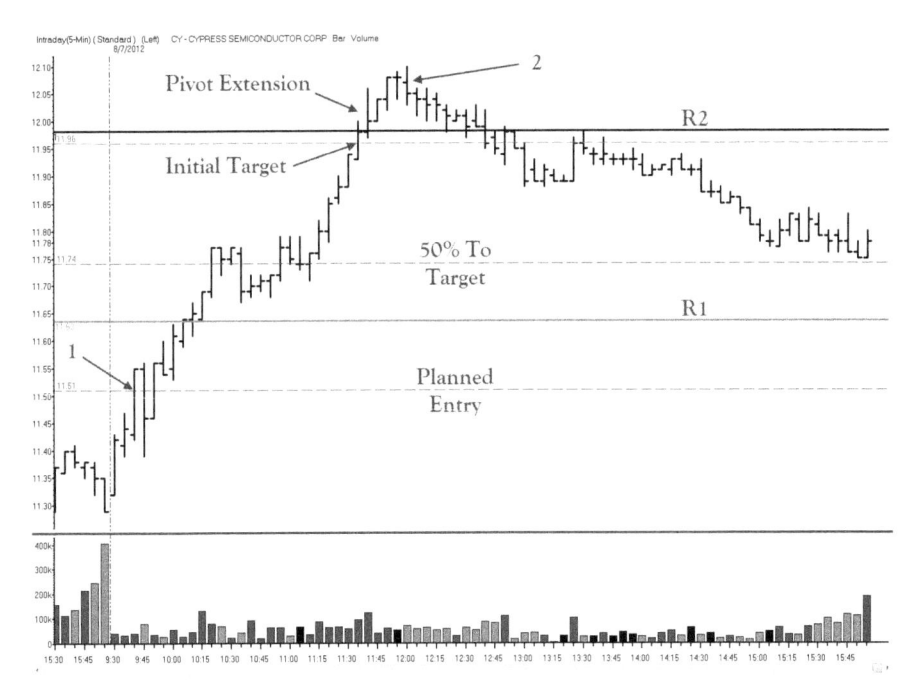

FIGURE 15.4 – CYPRESS SEMICONDUCTOR
RealTick by Townsend Analytics, Ltd.

Cypress Semiconductor (CY) opened flat and started trading higher. An entry was triggered according to the plan (1), and the upward move continued to the 50%-to-target level. At this point, the stop loss was moved to breakeven. When CY started moving again, it smoothly traded to the initial target and then made an extension move through the R2 pivot. A reversal of two closes triggered the exit for the trade, with a $0.10 extension of the initial profit target.

Around The Horn Plan
Thursday, August 09, 2012

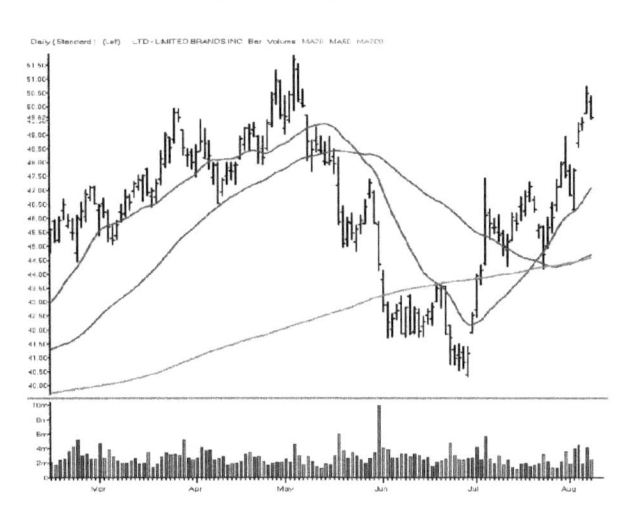

Symbol	LTD	Sector Symbol	$RLX.X
Description	LIMITED BRANDS INC		
Pattern	Kings And Queens	Apparel Retail	

Position	Short	Resistance 2	50.71
Entry	49.45	Resistance 1	50.16
Stop	49.79	Pivot	49.86
Initial Target	48.96	Support 1	49.31
Ratio	1.44	Support 2	49.01
50% To Target	49.21		

FIGURE 15.5

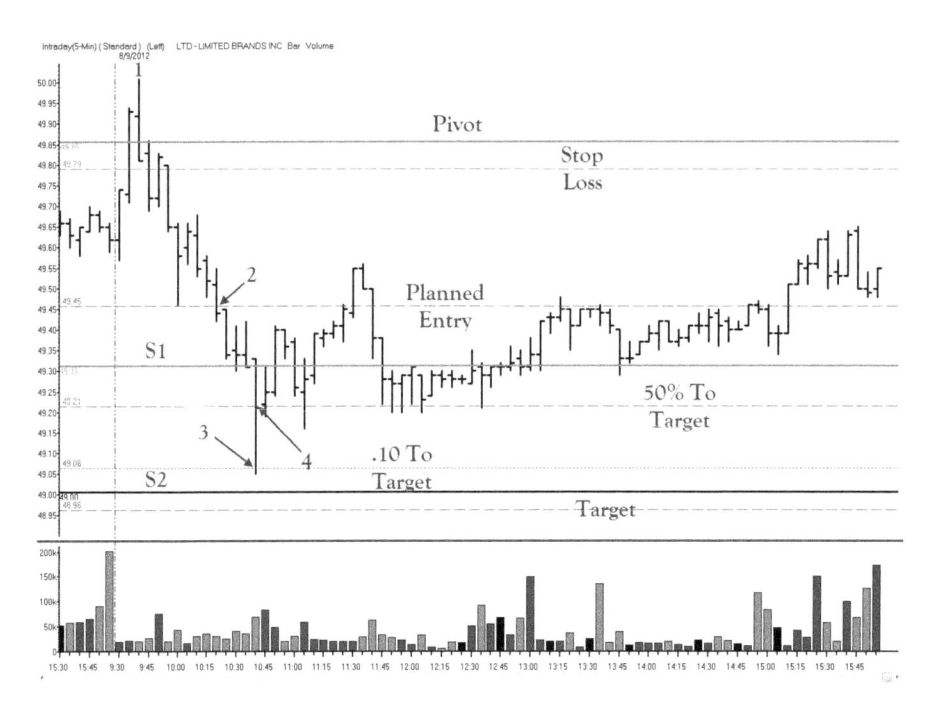

FIGURE 15.6 – LIMITED BRANDS
RealTick by Townsend Analytics, Ltd.

Limited Brands (LTD) offered us yet another early pivot entry when the stock opened flat, traded higher through the planned stop loss, moved higher through the central pivot, reversed, and triggered an entry (1). A stop on the position was placed .10 above the central pivot. A move lower through the planned entry price (2) triggered a doubling of the existing position (2). When LTD moved to the .10 to the target level, the stop was moved to the 50% to target line, per the rule book that accompanies the trading plan (3). A reversal in the same bar (4) stopped out the trade for a profit of $0.62 on the first leg of the trade, and $0.24 on the second leg. The net on the double lot was an average of $0.43 per share.

148 | Beat the Street

Around The Horn Plan
Wednesday, June 27, 2012

Symbol	MOS	Sector Symbol	$CEX.X
Description	MOSAIC CO NEW		
Pattern	Gap Extension	Fertilizers & Agricultural Chemicals	

Position	Long	Resistance 2	54.96
Entry	53.98	Resistance 1	54.13
Stop	53.51	Pivot	53.06
Initial Target	54.58	Support 1	52.23
Ratio	1.28	Support 2	51.16
50% To Target	54.28		

FIGURE 15.7

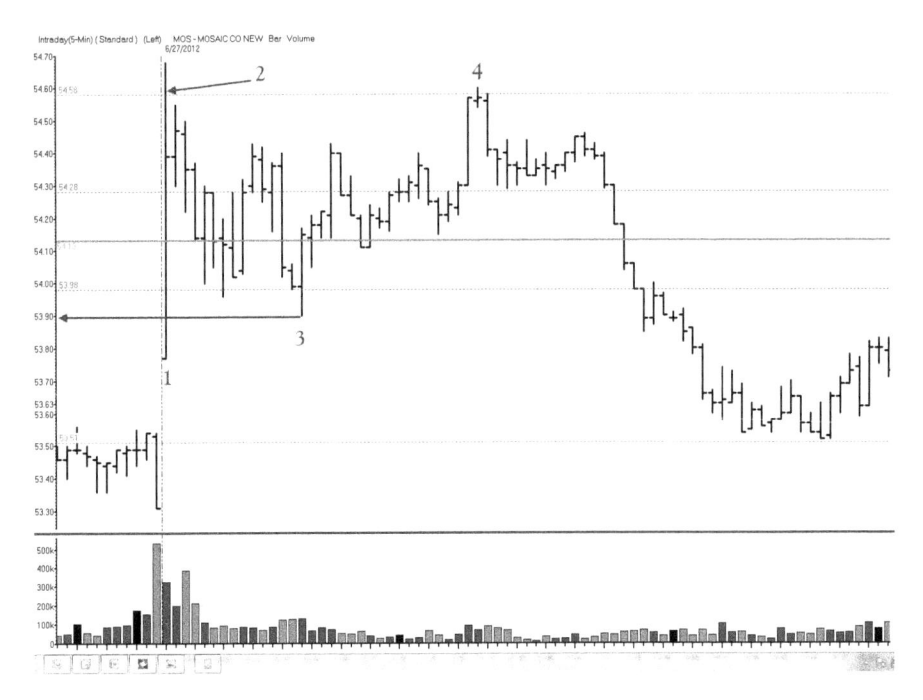

FIGURE 15.8 – MOSAIC
RealTick by Townsend Analytics, Ltd.

Mosaic (MOS) has been one of my favorite stocks to trade for several years. The volatility is generally in favour of the set-up momentum, and targets are achieved very quickly, minimising exposure and risk. Today was no exception, as the stock opened and triggered in the first two minutes of trading (1). By the time the first five-minute bar closed, MOS had achieved the initial target, booking a $0.60-per-share gain.

A reversal lower moved the stock through the .08 threshold in the rulebook, validating a second entry. The stock immediately traded higher triggering a second entry (3). I always take first and second entries automatically, and was rewarded when MOS moved to the target again, booking another $0.60-per-share gain.

Around The Horn Plan
Tuesday, March 13, 2012

Symbol	LII	Sector Symbol	SDJI
Description	LENNOX INTL INC		
Pattern	XRVC	Building Products	

Position	Long	Resistance 2	41.30
Entry	41.22	Resistance 1	41.11
Stop	40.79	Pivot	40.94
Initial Target	41.77	Support 1	40.75
Ratio	1.28	Support 2	40.58
50% To Target	41.50		

FIGURE 15.9

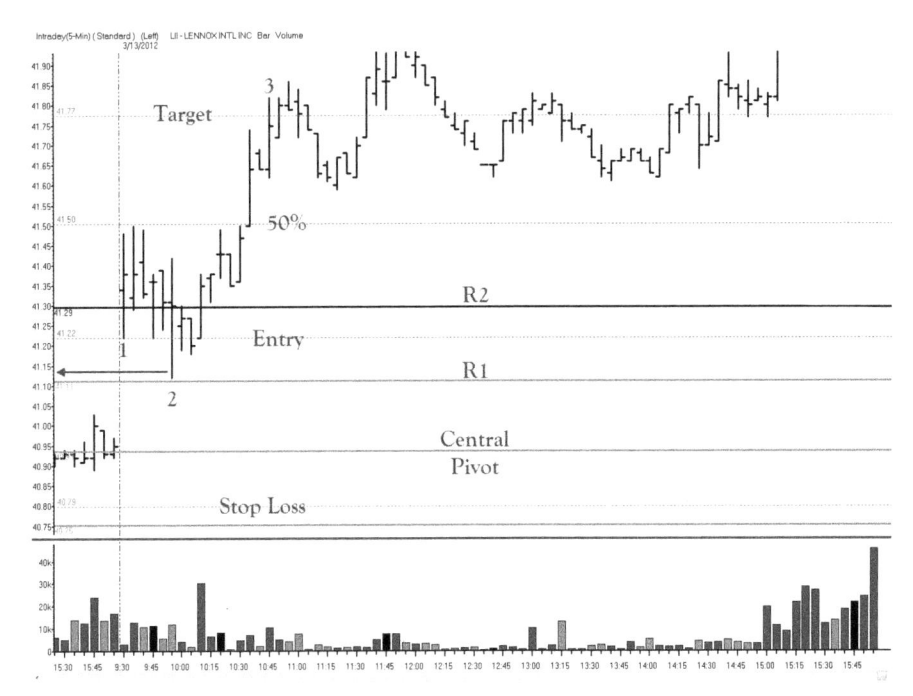

FIGURE 15.10 – LENNOX INTERNATIONAL INCORPORATED
RealTick by Townsend Analytics, Ltd.

Around The Horn Plan
Monday, March 12, 2012

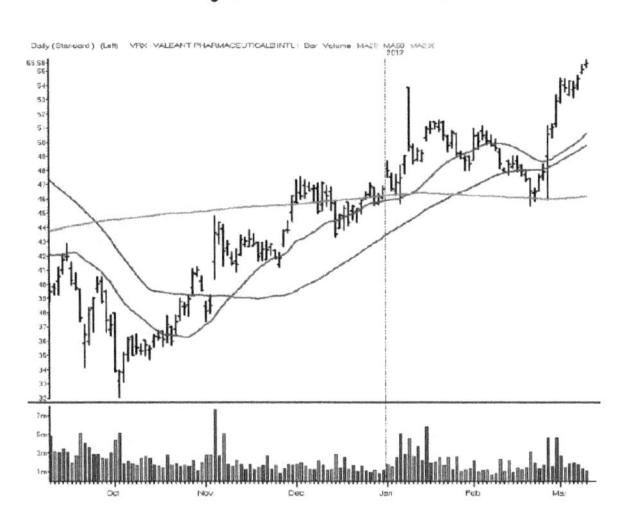

Symbol	VRX	Sector Symbol	$DRG.X
Description	VALEANT PHARMACEUTICALS INTL I		
Pattern	Extension Reversal	Pharmaceuticals	

Position	Short	Resistance 2	56.07
Entry	55.18	Resistance 1	55.83
Stop	55.47	Pivot	55.55
Initial Target	54.74	Support 1	55.31
Ratio	1.52	Support 2	55.03
50% To Target	54.96		

FIGURE 15.11

15. Keeping Score | **153**

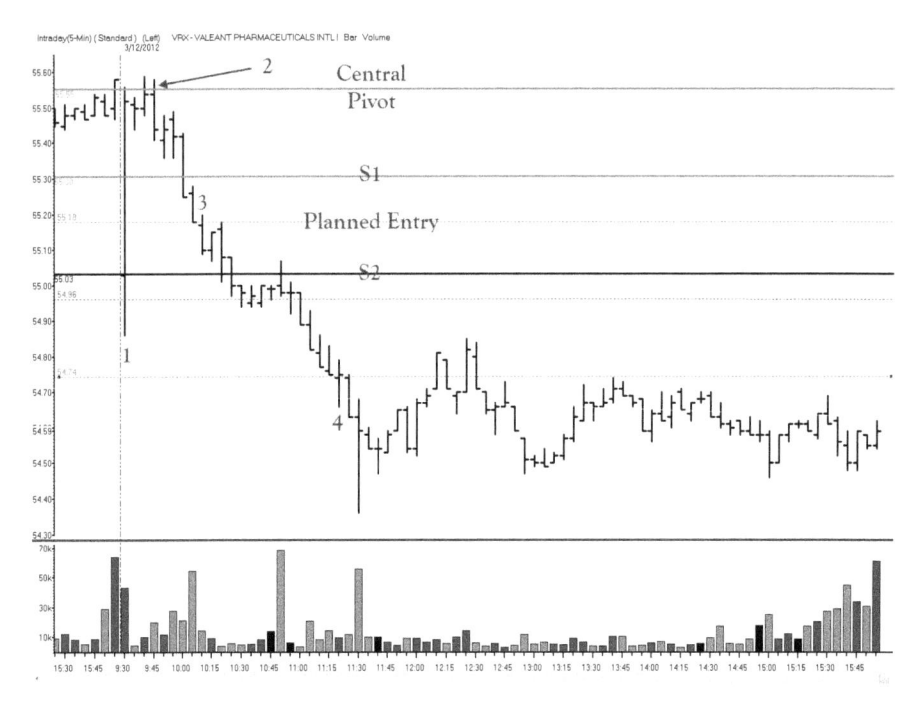

FIGURE 15.12 – VALEANT PHARMACEUTICALS
RealTick by Townsend Analytics, Ltd.

Valeant Pharmaceuticals (VRX) gapped lower to open at the 50% to target level (1). The stock then had a sharp reversal and moved higher to the central pivot. A reversal through the central pivot triggered an early entry with a tight, $0.10 stop loss (2). In 30 minutes, the stock moved lower to the planned entry, where I doubled my position (3). A smooth move lower triggered my exit at the initial target (4). In retrospect, a reversal-of-two-closes trailing stop would have kept me in the trade for a profit extension of a quarter point, and my exit was more a function of anticipation of trouble than of reaction to a valid signal.

Around The Horn Plan
Thursday, April 05, 2012

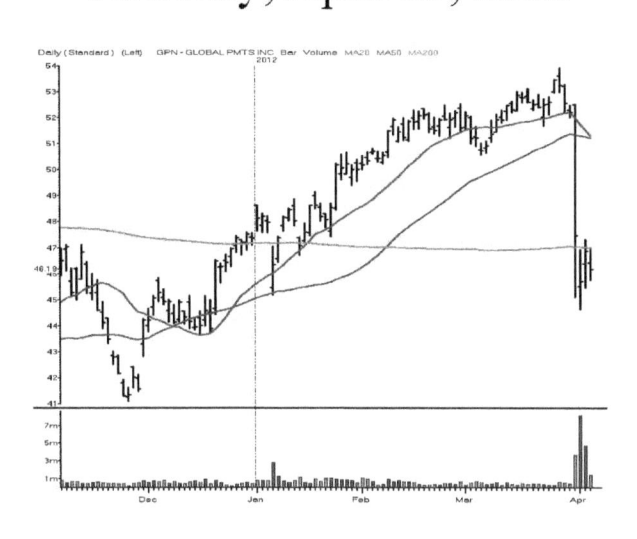

Symbol	GPN	Sector Symbol	$XIT.X
Description	GLOBAL PMTS INC		
Pattern	XRR	Data Processing & Outsourced Services	

Position	Short	Resistance 2	47.59
Entry	45.67	Resistance 1	46.89
Stop	46.16	Pivot	46.33
Initial Target	45.11	Support 1	45.63
Ratio	1.14	Support 2	45.07
50% To Target	45.39		

FIGURE 15.13

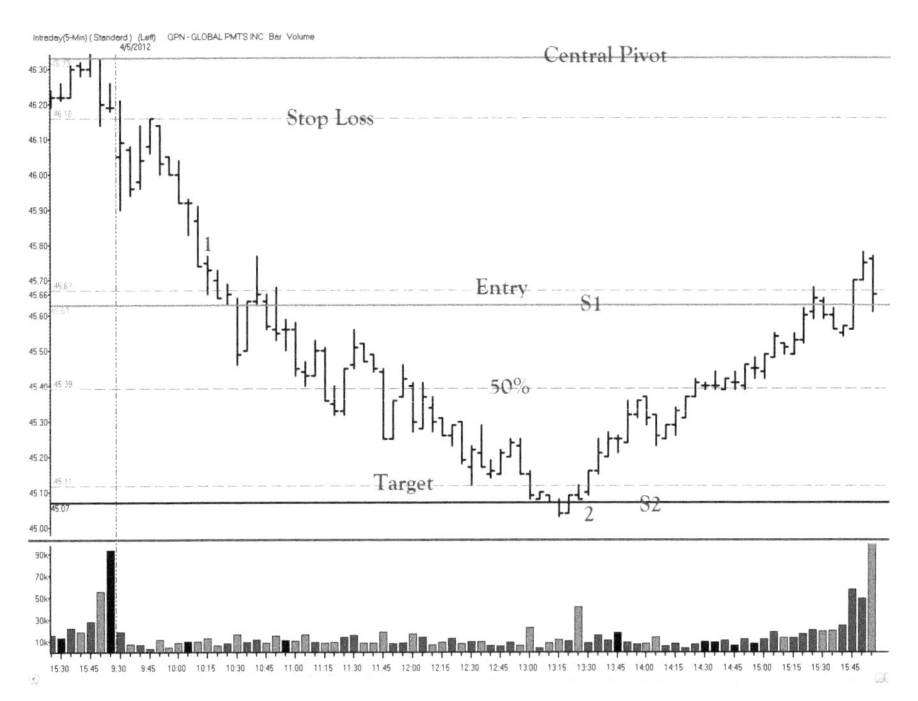

FIGURE 15.14 – GLOBAL PAYMENTS
RealTick by Townsend Analytics, Ltd.

Global Payments (GPN) opened flat and traded lower through the entry price. The trigger was at $45.67 (1). The stock traded lower through the target, and when a move through the S2 pivot reversed, an exit was triggered at the initial target of 45.11 (2).

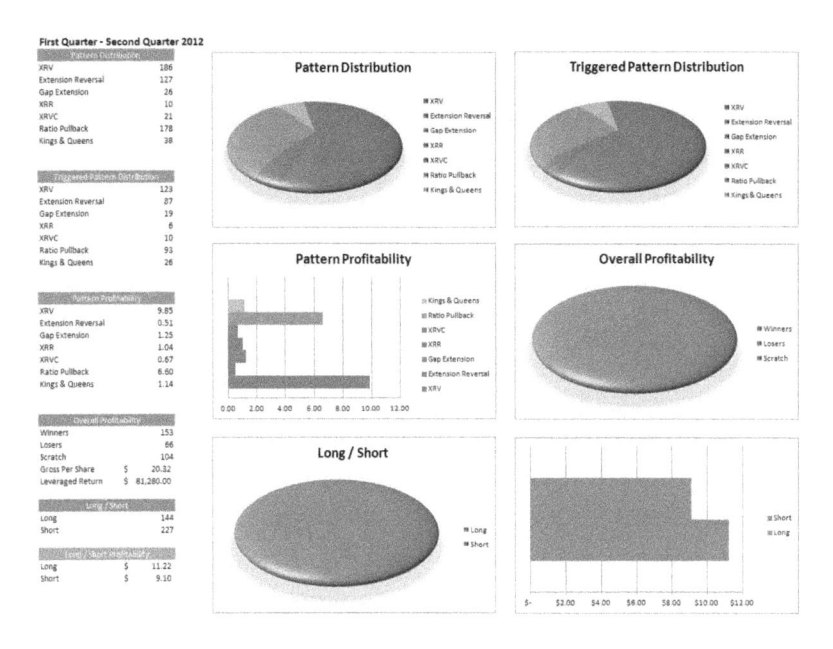

FIGURE 15.15

Analysing Results

Figure 15.15 is the actual first and second quarter 2012 summary from the analysis spreadsheet that I use to track my trading results. My trading software exports my daily trades via a data exchange and tracks the performance of every trade that triggered from my published *Around The Horn Intraday Trading Plan*. This allows me to carefully consider how each pattern is performing, and whether or not the cyclicality of the market is still reflected accurately in the distribution of pattern set-ups and triggers. Every trade represented in the spreadsheet was planned and published prior to the session for which profits or losses are recorded in Figure 15.15. The results are from set-ups just like, and including, those in Figures 15.1–15.14.

Looking at the data summaries for the first half of 2012, we see that the expansion of range and volume (XRV) presented a planned entry 186 times and triggered 123 trades in the first six months of the year. This is my core set-up, and it is not surprising to see it dominate the distribution. What is important to me is that it

15. Keeping Score | 157

also dominates the profitability distribution. I would be alarmed if my most frequently occurring trade did not generate the majority of my profits. In the case of the XRV, $9.85 per share traded or 9.85% was the profit that the pattern contributed to the bottom line for a $100,000 account trading a fixed 1,000 share lot size. In this $100,000 trading account, this would translate into $9,850. If the same account was deploying more capital for each trade, and trading 2,000 shares, the return would be $19,700 or 19.7%. Looking down the lefthand column, we see the results for each of the patterns in this book. In terms of overall profitability, each of the patterns generated positive results in the first half of 2012.

The ratio of winners to losers, and winners to scratched trades, is also of great interest to me. In Chapter 3, I discussed the 50% scratch stop, and the fact that if a trade moves 50% of the distance from the entry to the target and then retraces to the entry, I close out the position at the entry price for no gain or loss. I generally expect that the proportions of 50% scratch stops and stop losses in my spreadsheet will be approximately equal. This lets me know that the rules of my trading plan are working in my favour. I do quarterly analyses of this ratio by looking at the individual trades to ascertain what happened after the 50% scratch stop was triggered. I home in on the number of times that the trades would have gone on to the full stop loss after my exit, and I am pleased to say that the 50% scratch stop has protected profitability significantly.

The long to short ratio is another metric that I am extremely interested in. In Figure 15.15, we see that fewer long trades than short trades were taken in the first half of 2012. We also see that the longs generated more profits than the shorts. This tells me that either the market has signalled and triggered many false reversal entries, or that I am allowing a short-side bias to enter my decision-making process when planning my trades. I make adjustments to my thinking if the latter is true.

The effect of trade size is why I generally do not represent the results of my set-ups as percentages. Every trader has a different account size, risk profile and trading history. Therefore percentage return can be misleading. A smaller account of $25,000, trading a larger share size will generate a larger percentage return, even though the points, or dollars per share, and actual dollars earned are identical to those in the $100,000 account. In the $25,000 account, trading 1,000 shares, the XRV would return $9,850 or 39% to the account. Trading 2,000 shares and generating $19,700 would result in a gain of 78.8%. In both cases, the absolute value of the dollars returned to the account are identical to those generated in the $100,000 account, but the percentage return is amplified in the smaller account. You can see how account size can be used to manipulate results. I hope that readers will bear this in mind the next time they run across someone who claims to have returned 1,000% over the course of a few days or trades.

There are extensive free support resources for readers of *Beat the Street* at **www.traderinsight.com**, and I strongly encourage you to check the site for updates every day. The results for every month since 2005, along with quarterly and yearly summaries, are available in the free member area. Videos of actual trades being taken, along with strategy reviews, are also available there. The free videos also show you many alternative entry techniques, scalping strategies and money management rules that I apply to actual trades. The examples make the ideas presented in this book come to life, and add clarity and insight that cannot be gained just by reading a text. The extensive results available at the site demonstrate the power of the approach presented here, and should make readers confident that a thorough understanding of what is presented in this book can be the cornerstone of a profitable trading business. There have been no losing months since 2005. All patterns have been profitable in each of the yearly summaries. These facts alone say a great deal about what can be accomplished by successfully implementing my trading strategies.

Summary

I provided the examples in this section for the purpose of clarifying how I keep records. I suggest that you keep at least as much historical information about your trading activity as I do. The preference would be that you keep even more. There is no such thing as too much information when it comes to evaluating our own decisions and emotions. I hope that this section has given you a good place from which to start.

CHAPTER 16.
Closing Thoughts

Well, there you have it. You now possess some of the insight that a decade of trading professionally has brought me. The strategies I use are predominantly straightforward. Most trace their origins back to the earlier part of the last century when people like Gann were writing the book on technical analysis. Since that time, these set-ups have worked for traders through bull and bear markets, just as I am certain they shall continue to generate profits in the future.

I rely on money management to keep my business profitable. I only plan to take a trade if it has at least a 1:1 profit/loss ratio. Before I accept even these odds of success, I make sure that the stock I am dealing with is heading in a direction supported by its fundamentals, and is unencumbered by intraday support and resistance.

I believe that consistency is the key to success as an equities trader. I don't do a lot of flip-flopping when it comes to strategies. I trade the patterns in this book every day. If you find that they fit your personal psychology, I would suggest that you add them to your repertoire slowly. Get to know each strategy; make sure it makes sense to you before you add additional ones. For further examples of the set-ups, check **www.traderinsight.com** regularly. There you will find daily examples of the *Beat the Street* patterns my wife Julie and I are currently trading. You can also listen to my nightly audio commentary and read my daily watchlist to help you with the next day's trading. The stocks I discuss at **www.traderinsight.com** are the very same ones that I will be looking to trade. Go to the site today, and be sure to sign up for my free newsletter. I'll email you new trading ideas, set-ups and actionable market information every day.

You can also look over our shoulder in the War Room, an interactive community full of educational opportunities and live commentary from a variety of well-known professional traders. We run the online war room from our personal war room regularly, and readers always love spending the day with us and seeing the ideas in *Beat the Street* come to life. A question that comes up in every session regards what technology we use in our trading. As it is always of interest to traders of all levels of development, I would like to answer that question here.

Our war room is pictured below. As you can see, we use eleven screens to monitor the markets over the course of the day. This gives us plenty of room to watch what each of the stocks in the nightly service is doing.

We use two Alienware workstations at the highest clock speed available today to run our trading business. Each of the machines is loaded with more RAM and more hard disk space than we will likely use in a lifetime. I am a firm believer in headroom, and the machine you make your living with should be a best-in-class, highly reliable product. These are gaming machines with incredible graphics and processing capabilities. No games are installed on either machine, however, as we make our living in the greatest game ever – trading.

I use RealTick for analysis, plan preparation and trading. The data and execution capabilities available in RealTick are without question the best in the industry.

Finally, if you are new to this business, I suggest that you read everything you can. Attend seminars, watch educational programmes about trading, and scour the internet until you find a methodology that you think suits you. Every one of us can find a method that helps us become a successful trader. None of us can do so by blindly following the first methodology that comes along. Make sure that the fit between your belief structure and that of the system you are adopting is tight. Only then will you be able to trade confidently and in a manner that increases your chances of success.

I know from personal experience what you are up against in the profession you have chosen; if you find your own way to rise above it all, I am confident that choosing it shall be the best decision you ever made. I wish you good luck on your journey.

Good Trading,

ADRIAN MANZ

You can find great *Beat the Street* trading set-ups every day at **TraderInsight.com**

Every evening, I post *Beat the Street* stock trading set-ups at **www.traderinsight.com**. At the same site you can listen to my nightly audio commentary and read my daily watchlist to help you with the next day's trading. These stocks are the very same ones that I will be looking to trade. Go to the site today, and be sure to sign up for my free newsletter. I'll email you new trading ideas, set-ups and actionable market information.

Take your trading to the next level with
Trade Secrets

- Completely updated sequel to *Beat the Street*.
- All-new examples, featuring recent market movements and example stock picks relevant for the markets of today and the future.
- Go in-depth on the expansion-of-range-and-volume set-up.
- Master volatility with exclusive, powerful strategies used on a daily basis by Adrian Manz.
- Another cult trading classic from Harriman House.

www.harriman-house.com/tradesecrets